THOMAS ECCLESHARE: PLAYS ONE

Thomas Eccleshare

PLAYS ONE

OBERON BOOKS
LONDON

WWW.OBERONBOOKS.COM

First published in 2019 by Oberon Books Ltd
521 Caledonian Road, London N7 9RH
Tel: +44 (0) 20 7607 3637 / Fax: +44 (0) 20 7607 3629
e-mail: info@oberonbooks.com
www.oberonbooks.com

PB ISBN: 9781786827609
E ISBN: 9781786827623

Cover image: Róger Zambrano

Printed and bound by 4EDGE Limited, Hockley, Essex, UK.

Visit www.oberonbooks.com to read more about all our books and to buy them. You will
also find features, author interviews and news of any author events, and you can sign up
for e-newsletters and be the first to hear about our new releases.

Printed on FSC® accredited paper

10 9 8 7 6 5 4 3 2 1

For my parents

Contents

Introduction

U nlike a lot of playwrights, my background is in mime. I trained at the Jacques Lecoq school, I have a company (Dancing Brick) that makes visual theatre and quite a few of my shows have been completely silent. Which is why, by way of explaining a little bit about my process as a writer and despite the fact that this is a book filled almost exclusively with dialogue, I want to start by considering mime.

By considering a mimed, let's say... bottle.

A mimed bottle is better than a real bottle onstage because it allows – *requires* – the audience to give something of themselves to the completion of the image. In doing so they become, in a profound way, intermingled with it and inseparable from it.

With mime, this collaboration between the performer and the audience is as intense as it is delicate. You have to inspire the audience's imagination by pressing at the edges of things or by tracing the outlines of things, but it is up to them to fill in the rest of the space themselves. The bottle cannot exist without both of you.

To bring a real bottle onstage is an act of selfishness; it is saying 'I know this bottle better than you can imagine it'. The only excuse for bringing a real bottle onstage is to allow the audience to use their imaginations elsewhere or in different ways – to say 'let me handle the bottle, you get busy thinking about something more interesting'.

The plays in this book aren't mime shows (sidebar: what would *that* book look like?), but even when I'm writing plays like these ones, built on words and dialogue, I always try to give the audience the space to imagine their own bottle.

For me, the principal pleasure of going to the theatre is using your imagination, so it's my job as a theatre maker to inspire that. But it's a balance. Everything that the audience sees or hears onstage is one *less thing* they get to imagine, which is why it's so boring to see a fully naturalistic set, or to see a play with a 'message'. Having said that, if you don't put *enough* onstage then the audience have to do *too much* work and you run the risk of them getting bored. In one of Dancing Brick's shows we had a twenty minute-long mime sequence of a woman suffering from Alzheimer's disease making a cup of tea, twice. For me that was a beautiful and heartbreaking thing to sink into and inspired a lot of imagination whenever I watched it. For most of the audience: not so much.

This balance – between giving too much and too little – is the central and most important challenge for the playwright and goes to the heart of the relationship between the writer and the audience.

Let's imagine a theatre. You are sitting in the auditorium, looking at an empty stage. You are excited because in that empty space anything – *anything!* – is possible.

Into this space comes me, the writer, and I am dragging with me two pieces of scenery: a bar stool and a sign, upon which is written 'Frank's Bar'.

Immediately, I have cut off a trillion possibilities for you. No longer could this space be a zoo, or a church, or 'Tony's Bar'; now, this space is 'Frank's Bar'. This is a dick move from me, because I am depriving you of your ability to imagine something other than Frank's bar. I am funnelling you into a bar of my own choosing.

But this is the balance I have to strike. I know that simply leaving the space empty for an hour and a half will quite quickly (or, depending on your taste, quite slowly) get boring. I have to inspire your imaginations somehow. I have conjured 'Frank's Bar' to do this. Perhaps, I hope, if I bring enough things into Frank's bar, or the right characters or the right words coming from those characters in that bar then you will imagine or feel or learn (ugh!) things you could never have imagined on your own.

But I have to be careful. Because whilst bringing nothing onstage would get boring, it would be even worse if I brought too much. Everything I bring onstage, every character I name, every place I specify, fills in a bit more of that lovely empty space. If I'm not careful there will be no space left for your imagination, and then I might as well be here on my own.

In my work then, in order to facilitate as much imagining as possible for the audience, I try to create 'gaps'. Gaps are the spaces into which the audience is able to pour their imagination. These gaps might be stylistic (a mimed bottle instead of a real one) or narrative (why does Frank not work at his bar any more?) or formal (three distinct acts) or even just typographic (setting the scenes in different rooms in *Instructions,* with no explicit explanation of what that might look like onstage).

A good illustration of this principal, in this case applied to character, is that when Shakespeare adapted *King Lear* from his source material, he deliberately *removed* Lear's wife. By carving out this gap he creates questions to which we can provide our own (inevitably more interesting) answers – who is the mother of these women? Where is she now? What happened to her?

It comes down to remembering this: the audience will always be more interesting than me.

And now, with Shakespeare well and truly lodged in your mind as a point of comparison, I'll talk a bit about my plays.

After graduating from Lecoq I formed a company with Valentina Ceschi. Together, we made (and still make) work that was written 'in the room'; maybe by improvisation, maybe by playing around with a costume, maybe by cobbling together a mask. Things are changing, but even now there is a hierarchy in England between theatre that is written collaboratively – 'devised' – and theatre that is written by a solitary genius, alone in her flat. Riled by this hierarchy, after a couple of years of making and touring our work, I tried to write a play by typing at a keyboard.

There were two main reasons I think I did this. Firstly, I was somewhat bitterly courting respect from traditional seats of theatre power like the Royal Court and I felt that writing this sort of play was the only way I could get it. Secondly, I wanted the freedom to not have to produce the idea.

When Valentina and I made work, we had to find a way to realise the wild things we thought of. This is brilliant most of the time, indeed that challenge is an integral part of the creative process. But there is something freeing about seeing a blank page and thinking 'all I have to do is write it – it's up to someone *else* to work out how to stage it'. Which is basically how I started *Pastoral*. I had an image in my head, of a tree growing through the floor of a stage. I didn't know how it got there or what was happening. So I wrote the play to find out.

Even though *Pastoral* was my first 'play' written in this way, it actually felt like a very familiar process to the shows I had made before. In theatre the word 'writing' (when used as a noun) is often used interchangeably with the word 'dialogue', but this is reductive. I have made two completely silent mime shows but the process of making them felt no less like 'writing' than the plays here. The requirements – of structure, of tonal control, of characterisation – are more or less the same no matter how the theatre is made. The text – the spoken words – is just one of many component parts that come together to make a piece of theatre, alongside the body, the music, the costumes, the set, the audience and of course many more. In fact one of the things I am most interested in doing is exploring ways in which these component parts can be isolated and the relationships between them exploded. Which is kind of how *I'm Not Here Right Now* came about; by wanting to experiment with separating the words from the image, and seeing what that gap did for the audience.

As it turned out, the answer to that question was a combination of 'annoyed them' and 'made them very bored'.

I'm Not Here Right Now took a fucking kicking. I've never been involved in a show that got worse reviews. And, to be fair, worse audience reactions. You know when you're performing a show if it's landing with the audience and you know when it's missed. And this definitely missed. I thought when I came back to it that I would see why, that the flaws in it would reveal themselves as huge and obvious and I would see why the audience lost interest or got annoyed. I was actually worried to read it again because I thought I would be embarrassed. But you know what, it might be my favourite of these plays. It's an experiment in form and it tries to do something that interests me – separate out the *material* of the theatre (in this case the text and the image) and play around with that separation. In doing so I think its form and its content have interesting things to say about the gaps between what we see and what we're told; between what we know and what we feel; and, most theatrically, between the 'real' and the 'imagined'. I find the way the form and content come together at the end moving and surprising and successful. Unfortunately, no one else agreed with me!

Heather was inspired by a conversation I had with my brother and sister. We were listening to Tracy Chapman and talking about whether it would make any difference to the music if we found out that the singer was actually a posh white girl from Finchley. Simultaneous to that I was working on a film set in a prison and meeting a lot of inmates; the experience was intense and fascinating; getting to like and respect these men without knowing what they'd done and then, in some cases, finding out. Unlike the other plays here, *Heather* didn't start with a stage image, but with a 'what if'; a case of knowing the story a little bit, and then just improvising around it. Of all the work I've ever made, *Heather* was the quickest and easiest to write. I tried adding bits and pieces to it at times (there was once an introductory part, and a second act with a journalist) but in the end I liked the lack of explanation between each act and, as I said above, adding more just seemed to give the audience less space.

Like *I'm Not Here Right Now, Heather* was another attempt to deconstruct certain component parts of the theatre form, in this case the actor from the character. Because the play is so much about authorship and whether it matters who is speaking, I wanted to exploit the fact that the relationship between actor and character usually goes completely unchallenged in the mind of the audience.

Heather is a good example of the gaps I was speaking about earlier. I tried to prise the gaps as wide open as possible; so for example the gaps between the acts are formally quite large and as a result the audience is given a lot of freedom to build their own bridges between them.

Looking over my notes for *Instructions For Correct Assembly* I found something that I wrote on one of my first days of writing: 'let it always be plastic and flat and without depth, the better to conceal the depths that they are hiding'. Again, this was about creating a gap, really – between the seemingly optimistic, 'can-do' attitude that Max and Hari are projecting, and the depth of hurt behind. As an audience member I rarely find it sad when actors deliver big, tearful monologues expressing all the *pain* they are feeling (again – where is my space to *imagine* their pain, to give a part of myself to it?) Much sadder when they try to keep smiling and insist everything is fine.

I came to think of *Instructions* as a 'flatpack play'; where the scattered accumulation of scenes would come together to make something beautiful. In fact, Max's line towards the beginning was intended as a bit of an instruction for the audience: 'It's all these bits. You're looking at them and thinking ok this doesn't make any sense and I wouldn't have thought that that went there or in that order but then two hours later once it's all come together you're looking at it and thinking: wow.'

I wrote it on attachment at the Royal Court. Opposite the theatre is a big department store and I would go there and walk through the different floors and basically write a scene in each different showroom. In that way I think of it as a bit of a site specific play – specific to the home furnishings department of John Lewis.

Like *Pastoral*, I began with an image I wanted to see onstage. In this case, it was a man unscrewing the back of a silent boy's head, fiddling around, pressing a button, and then the boy talks. That was the beginning of the writing and everything else came as a surprise to me. My feeling is: if it is surprising to me, then hopefully it will be surprising to the audience.

These are some of the plays I've written so far in my life. Thank you for reading them and I hope you find them moving, entertaining and inspiring.

TCE, 2019

PASTORAL

Pastoral was first performed at Soho Theatre on 25th April 2013 in a co-production with HighTide Festival and featured the following cast and creative team:

MOLL	Anna Calder-Marshall
HARDY	Richard Riddell
MANZ	Hugh Skinner
ARTHUR	Polly Frame
MR. PLUM	Nigel Betts
MRS. PLUM	Morag Siller
OCADO MAN	Bill Fellows
THE BRIDE	Carrie Rock

Directed by	Steve Marmion
Designed by	Michael Vale
Lighting by	Philip Gladwell
Music and sound by	Tom Mills

Characters

MOLL, *a very old woman*

HARDY, *a man, twenties*

MANZ, *a man, twenties*

ARTHUR, *an eleven-year-old boy*

MR. PLUM, *his father*

MRS. PLUM, *his mother*

OCADO MAN

THE BRIDE

1.

A small flat with all the furniture removed. A door to the bathroom, a door to the bedroom and a front door to the hall. Upstage is a kitchenette with a window. On the window ledge are some flowers in a vase.

Grass, leaves and weeds are growing through the floorboards and under the doors.

In the only chair in the flat sits MOLL. By the door are two packed cases.

MOLL takes her handbag and slowly opens it.

Out of the handbag flies a fly. MOLL swipes at it and it disappears. She looks around her.

From her handbag she removes a compact mirror. She checks herself in the mirror. She replaces the mirror and withdraws from the bag a stick of lipstick, which she applies. Once finished she replaces the lipstick and checks the compact mirror again. She replaces the compact mirror and removes a tube of mascara from the bag, which she applies, carefully to each eye and then, having finished, checks the mirror. She replaces the compact mirror.

She removes from the bag an opened packet of pre-packaged fruit (anything that has been pre-sliced or pre-peeled will do). She eats the last of the fruit and places the empty pack in her bag.

She goes to the kitchenette. She picks up a food processor and places it in a large cardboard box. She opens a drawer, takes out an electric whisk and puts it in the cardboard box too. She unplugs the toaster on the kitchen top and puts it into the box. The kitchen is now bare.

She looks out of the window.

She looks back.

MOLL   Everyone out there is fat.

5

She looks out again.

Except…no, that's a lamp-post. Everyone out there is fat. There's four fat women, two fat men, five fat children and a fat infant. Suckling on her fat mum's breast. It's one of those milky, floppy breasts.

She mimes the breast.

She chuckles.

They're trying to jog. Bless them.

She takes a long sip of her tea.

She looks out again.

There's also a dog. A fat dog.

Pause.

Don't get me wrong, I've got nothing against the fat. Apart from on buses and planes. Or in lifts. Or in sexual situations, apart from with one another. I wouldn't want to get into a sexual situation with a fat. Not even on top. Imagine being in a sexual situation with a fat. Imagine it. It would be like being humped by a bouncy castle. A fat man: The breasts that flop. The wobbly flesh. The search for his prick in amongst the folds of wibbly flab. *(She mimes a bit.)* Having to flatten it out like a space on the beach so you can lie down.

A sip of tea.

No thanks.

She looks out again, this time for a bit longer.

6

Midsummer Place. A *place*. A *piazza*. Boots, Nandos, Gourmet Burger Kitchen. Zizzi. *(Enjoying the word, flirting.)* Zzzzizzi. I've not been.

Ever had a fat? Well exactly. I don't know how they reproduce.

A glance out.

Costa coffee's still open. A fat family sitting outside. *Al Fresco.* Like hippos in a swamp. They're being moved on.

I've got an order coming. Ocados. Bringing me my shopping. The good thing about Ocados is they'll shove it in colour coded bags. Cupboard, fridge...there's another one too. Cupboard, fridge. Red, purple...green. What's green? Anyway, Ocados're coming any minute with my weeklies.

(Looks out. Looks back at public, disgusted.) I mean fucking hell.

She drinks her tea.

Winston?... Pss, pss. Winston...?

Freezer! That's it.

She goes to the kitchen and gets a pre-packed cat food portion from a cupboard. She pulls off the silver foil sleeve and puts it on the floor.

She waits.

Last one. No more for Winston, no more for me.

Winston?

She looks out of the window again.

The family's gone.

There's another one though, outside the Häagen Dazs café. Skinny boy and two round parents. It's like they've been inflated.

Everything's growing.

Winston?

Silly mog.

There's a key in the door.

MANZ enters.

MANZ   Are you ready? Jesus, it's up here already.

MOLL   Was there anyone downstairs?

MANZ   No, they've gone.

MOLL   I told you. Everyone's going.

MANZ   Don't talk like that. They'll come back.

MOLL   How do you know?

MANZ   They left a note.

MOLL   Really? What did it say?

MANZ   They've gone on holiday. Just for a bit.

MOLL   Where to?

MANZ   Guernsey. Are you packed?

MOLL   I saw them leave.

MANZ   Moll.

MOLL   They had a lot of stuff.

MANZ	It's an adventure holiday. You need equipment.
MOLL	A couple of car loads at least.
MANZ	They're going potholing. You need all sorts for that. Come on.
MOLL	What's potholing?
MANZ	Hardy will be here soon and he'll want to be off.
MOLL	Is it like pottery?
MANZ	Have you packed?
MOLL	Or like pot?
MANZ	Moll?
MOLL	Or like moling?
MANZ	Moll. Are you ready?
MOLL	Nearly.
MANZ	Good girl. Don't look out there, it'll get your heart going. *(He sees the flowers.)* Christ!
	He goes to the vase and tips the flowers out of the window. He washes the vase thoroughly then, thinking better of it, throws the vase out of the window too.
	I'll help you finish packing up.
MOLL	Alright.
MANZ	What's left?
MOLL	A lot of the kitchen.
MANZ	Right.
MOLL	And the bathroom.
MANZ	Oh.

MOLL	And most of my bedroom.
MANZ	So what is done?
MOLL	I took care of Winston's basket.
MANZ	You sit down, I'll get started.
MOLL	Why did you say to pack the kitchen stuff? Doesn't Claire have kitchen stuff?
MANZ	She wants you to be comfortable.
MOLL	I don't mind borrowing hers. It would save me packing and repacking.
MANZ	She just wants you to be at ease.
MOLL	Well that's the idea of a holiday.
MANZ	Exactly.
MOLL	Does Claire not have furniture at her place?
MANZ	The furniture's different. It's going into storage.
MOLL	Storage? Just for while I'm away?
MANZ	That's what people do now. They rent their furniture when they go away, to fund the trip.
MOLL	Who hires furniture?
MANZ	Restaurants, hospitals, that sort of thing.
MOLL	And you said it was delivered alright?
MANZ	Come away from the window, it's scary for you out there.
MOLL	We could have left the furniture here.
MANZ	It's no trouble.
MOLL	They said you could collect it any time you liked?

MANZ	And we'll bring it back here just like it was.
MOLL	I tried cutting a few of the weeds.
MANZ	Hardy told you not to bother yourself with them. Let the army deal with all of this. They'll clean it up. I told you what they did in Southampton. I showed you the pictures didn't I? It was as good as new.
MOLL	A man came round on Tuesday.
MANZ	Which man?
MOLL	He said he was looking for you or Hardy.
MANZ	Oh. It must have been a friend.
MOLL	He wanted me to confirm that you and Hardy looked after me. I told him. I said we were related.
MANZ	That will be Jack. He's always playing practical jokes on us. Once he pretended that Hardy had been kidnapped. Tried to get me to pay a ransom. He's hilarious.
MOLL	Simms, it said on his card. He was an estate agent.
MANZ	Jack Simms. Yes, Hardy knows him. He probably thought Hardy would be here.
MOLL	He said Hardy had told him to come and have a look round and tell him what he thought.
MANZ	He's proud of you.
MOLL	Give him an evaluation.
MANZ	Look Moll. Things are dangerous here for you now. Everyone else in the building's leaving if they haven't already left. I'll take you to Mum's.

	It's safe there. She's concreted the field outside and built plastic walls around the concrete. It's all the latest stuff. You'll be happy there. And then, in a few weeks, once the army sort this mess out, we can come back here. It doesn't hurt to know what you're worth.
MOLL	There are butterflies in the sink. I think they're nesting. I told Simms and he didn't seem too pleased about it. Do you know Simms?
MANZ	He's Hardy's friend.
MOLL	He looks like a condom.
MANZ	I'm nearly done here. Why don't you relax on your chair while I finish the rest?
MOLL	I didn't go to my drawing class on Thursday.
MANZ	What? Why not?
MOLL	That branch had grown through the hall overnight. I couldn't climb over it.
MANZ	You mean you stayed here?
MOLL	Yes.
MANZ	You were here all morning?
MOLL	Yes. Simms dropped round again. He had a key. He said Hardy had given it to him as he wanted to show some people the flat. A young black couple. He was surprised to see me. I said they were welcome to look around and were they looking for something similar? They said yes. Simms talked about the army too, about how they'd clean up all the branches and leaves. Clear the square again. Which was a relief.

MANZ	It's just a precaution Moll. In case these weeds don't get sorted out. In case you can't come back. It's just in case. Have a rest.

MANZ goes to clear the bathroom. He clatters around.

MOLL goes to make tea. It's the final teabag. She looks out of the window again.

MOLL   They first noticed it a few weeks ago, creeping round the war memorial and through the crack outside Subway. Just little weeds at first, little sprouts. Herbs and reeds and wild mushrooms. It's amazing how quickly they're growing though, I have to admit that.

She puts the tea on.

Where's Ocados? I'd murder a Pepperami.

She looks out of the window.

They must be freezing. Though I suppose the blubber protects them a bit. Why haven't they moved on? Someone should tell them it's dangerous. Everyone's moving. Maybe they can't lift themselves up.

Pause.

I'm working on a joke.

I've got the punchline, it's just a matter of working out the first bit. Well, not so much the punchline, but I know what I want to be the butt. The butt of the joke, I've got that all worked out. Hen nights. I've been thinking of one of those, 'such and such walked into a bar' formats.

A group of whales walk into a bar. *(Beat.)* It's a hen night.

Or, hang on. Seven drunk gorillas walk into a bar. *(Beat.)* It's a hen night. Hm. A number of drunk... A number of...

Needs work.

Knock knock. Who's there? Slags. Slags who? *(Pause.)* Just some slags on a hen night. Are at the front door.

It's coming.

Here's a hen night now, being shepherded through the square. Looks like it's over before it's begun. We get a lot of hen nights. And even more over the last week. Everyone's getting married. Flash weddings, like during a war. There's fifteen of them! Fifteen! Dressed in pink. Original. And they've got fairy wings. Optimistic to think those wings will get those bodies off the ground. You'd need a forklift truck.

Who've we got? They have names on the backs of their shirts, you see. 'Superslag', 'Attila the Slut', 'Queen Dicktoria', 'Pink Fairy', 'Lady Bra Bra'. 'Liz'. Not very imaginative, Liz. 'The Boobmonster', 'Boobatron', 'Baron Von Boob', 'Napoleon Bonatart'. You get the idea. And here's the bride! To be fair, she is a good looking girl. Blonde and firm in all the right places. And on her T-shirt, hold on, she's got a special message. 'Buy me a shot, 'cos I'm tying the knot'. That's so sweet. Oh, and on the back… 'I'm the hen. Ask me to lay an egg'. I'm not sure I even know what that means. Vodka Revolution's closed. No party for you.

MANZ re-enters with a filled-up case.

MANZ   Moll, please.

MOLL goes to the chair.

MANZ goes to the bedroom.

MOLL looks at herself again in her compact mirror. An ant crawls onto her hand. She watches it crawl over her finger for a bit, then brushes it onto the floor and stamps on it, hard.

She falls asleep.

There is a key in the door. HARDY enters.

He sees MOLL asleep.

MANZ re-enters.

MANZ   Well?

HARDY   I've got the van downstairs. I had to park in St Luke's; the car park here's been torn to shreds. There's a willow come straight through it, squirrels and birds everywhere.

MANZ   I saw a deer on my way here.

HARDY   We need to go.

MANZ   Do you think we should wake her?

HARDY   Give it ten minutes, then I will.

MANZ   Where are you going to go?

HARDY   Sophie's parents have a shower on the ground floor.

15

MANZ	And space?
HARDY	How much will she take?
MANZ	Do they have a garden?
HARDY	They've concreted it over. Then tarmacked the concrete. It will be night, soon. No sun. We should get there before sunrise; they'll be stronger in the sun.
MANZ	Which route are you taking?
HARDY	I'll go out over Radburton, head north up the A11.
MANZ	They just closed the A11.
HARDY	Not five minutes ago they hadn't.
	They get out their phones and check.
HARDY	Shit.
MANZ	She thinks she's going to stay with my mum. For a holiday.
HARDY	Good. *(To himself.)* I'll take the B road then. Shit.
MANZ	She'll be disappointed.
HARDY	She'll get over it. It's for her own good. I told you she should have left days ago. The whole of the South's gone. Have you seen London?
MANZ	I showed her an old picture of Southampton. Told her it was after the army had cleared up.
HARDY	Hope's good for her.
MANZ	She met Simms.
HARDY	It doesn't matter now. He can't do anything, it's too late.
MANZ	I saw a vole earlier.

HARDY	Where?
MANZ	Coming out of Paperchase. It was strutting.
HARDY	I believe it. There was a rabbit warren at the bottom of Aldi almost a week ago. I saw a rabbit by the yoghurts. I walked right up to it and it just sat there. We looked at each other but it didn't move. I got to less than a metre away before it darted. How did they get a warren into Aldi? No one did anything about it. No one ever does anything about anything.
MANZ	What could they have done?
HARDY	Re-tiled? Extermination? Poison? What do people normally do? What have we been doing?
MANZ	Who knows? We thought we had time. They've been too quick for us and now it's escalated.
HARDY	Even two days ago I was still eating fruit. I cut into an apple and it fell apart with worms and maggots. I was sick. Fell apart in my hand with worms and maggots.
MANZ	We should wake her.
HARDY	Everything teeming with life.
MANZ	I could take her, if you like.
HARDY	You? Where would you take her?
MANZ	I could take her to Mum's. It's further but she knows her at least.
HARDY	I'll take her. Is it night yet?

MANZ goes to the window.

MANZ	The moon's up. It's shining on the grass in the square; wood rush and reedmace sprouting through the cracks. Trees now too.
HARDY	Sycamore?
MANZ	Not yet. Ash and oak saplings over bluebells and wood sorrel. The pavement outside Nandos has cracked open and there's a brook. Herons, kingfishers and ragged pondweed.
HARDY	We need to go. *(Gently.)* Moll? Moll.
MOLL	*(Waking.)* I'm here.
HARDY	It's time to go. I've got the van downstairs. I'll carry you down alright.
MOLL	Where's Winston? I don't want to go without Winston.
HARDY	He'll be fine Moll, he'll be here when you get back.
MOLL	Still, I'd like to take him. Can't we take him?
MANZ	You go down to the van with Hardy Moll. I'll find Winston and bring him down with me.
MOLL	Alright. Isn't there time for me to have a quick bath?
HARDY	They're closing Grafton Road in half an hour. We have to go *now*.
MOLL	I'll just get my handbag. Ah! Ah! A spider! As big as my hand.
MANZ	I'll get it.
HARDY	Use a glass.
MOLL	Jesus. It has flesh on its legs!

MANZ	Where's it gone?
	They look for it.
HARDY	It must have crawled back where it came from.
MANZ	Spiders.
HARDY	Mice'll be next. Then badgers. Let's go.
MOLL	Well, goodbye flat. See you shortly. Good luck.
	There is a knock on the door.
MOLL	Ocados! I told you they'd come.
	MOLL goes to the door and opens it.
	Into the room walks a chubby young boy, ARTHUR, holding a toy knight's sword.
	He stands in the middle of the room, looking around.
	Silence.
MOLL	He looks too young to drive a van. What's your name?
ARTHUR	Arthur.
MOLL	Like the king?
ARTHUR	No.
MOLL	Is that your sword?
ARTHUR	Yes.
MOLL	What do you have a sword for?
ARTHUR	It's just a toy. It's not real.
MOLL	Where are your parents?
ARTHUR	Knocking on doors too.
MOLL	Are you selling something? Would you like me to buy something?

19

ARTHUR	No.
HARDY	Why are you knocking on doors? It's dangerous out there.
ARTHUR	My mum told me to.
HARDY	And who told her to? Was it the policemen?
ARTHUR	Yes.
HARDY	Where?
ARTHUR	Häagen Dazs.
MANZ	Why didn't you go home?
ARTHUR	Because we're going on an adventure away from home. It's my job to be brave and find a place to camp.
MOLL	Like a knight in shining armour.
ARTHUR	Yes.
MOLL	Well you can stay here.
MANZ	Moll. We have to try to leave ourselves.
HARDY	Why didn't you go to the other floors? The other towers?
ARTHUR	This is my special building. I'm supposed to try this building cos it's the biggest and I'm the bravest of us three.
HARDY	Didn't you try the floors below?
ARTHUR	They're all locked. I tried to break in but I couldn't. Do you have any crisps?
	MANZ is at the window.
MANZ	The army's in the square. The roots have come right through now, grass as high as the bollards. They've cordoned off the entrances.

20

HARDY	Shit.
MANZ	It's too late. They've roped off Arlington Way. They must have quarantined the whole block.
MOLL	Go and get your parents. Tell them you've found a special place to camp.

2.

i)

The same flat. The next evening.

A huge oak has burst through the floorboards. The leaves and grass under the doors and floor are longer and denser.

MOLL, HARDY, MANZ, ARTHUR and MR. and MRS. PLUM are there. MR. and MRS. PLUM are both plump. There is a plate with some biscuit crumbs on it.

Silence.

MOLL   At least it'll look nice in Autumn.

MRS. PLUM picks up the plate and licks it clean.

When she has thoroughly licked it she passes it to her husband. He takes it and gives it another licking. He places it on the floor.

MRS. PLUM takes it up again and begins to lick.

ARTHUR   Can we order a pizza?

MR. PLUM   I told you Moll's already got food on the way Arthur. It'll be here soon.

Pause.

HARDY   Manz and I should go down there.

MOLL   It must be the roads that are keeping them. I can see from here, the roads are at a standstill. I've got a big order, it'll be enough for all of us.

MANZ   Moll, no one's coming in or out. Not even Ocados.

MRS. PLUM   Are they usually prompt?

MOLL	They're usually very prompt. I can see though, it's chaos down there. I can see why they would be delayed.
MRS. PLUM	Perhaps you could call them. See if there's anything you can do?
HARDY	Everyone looked the other way. We should have been evacuating days ago.
MOLL	Things shot up. We've been ambushed.
MANZ	*(At the window now.)* The square's gone. I can actually see it growing.
MOLL	They only pedestrianised it a few years ago, when Eat was still Our Price. They needn't have bothered!
MANZ	It's a copse now. Ash and oak and hazel all densely packed in.
HARDY	What do you say Manz, let's go down?
MOLL	First it was just one, a few weeks ago, a sapling by the war memorial.
MANZ	I can't see the cobbles, just leaves and branches.
MOLL	The noise of the birds will keep me up. Not to mention the fucking squirrels.
	ARTHUR laughs.
MANZ	The glass in the front of Paperchase has been smashed through. A birch has come straight up through it in the space of an hour.
MR. PLUM	Perhaps we should try the stairs again?
ARTHUR	Where's uncle Tim? Is he at home still?
MRS. PLUM	Yes Arthur. He's safely at home.

ARTHUR	Why was Daddy trying to call him all the time?
MRS. PLUM	Daddy wanted to tell him what a fun time we're having here.
ARTHUR	Wouldn't he want to come on the adventure?
MRS. PLUM	Uncle Tim has a bad back. He wouldn't like this sort of adventure.
ARTHUR	Why were you crying before?
MRS. PLUM	That's enough Arthur. Here, why don't you play on your PSP for a bit?
ARTHUR	I've clocked it. It's boring now. Does she have internet?
MRS. PLUM	I don't know love, why don't you ask her yourself. Politely.
ARTHUR	Excuse me. Have you got internet?
MRS. PLUM	Internet what?
ARTHUR	Sorry. Wireless internet.
MRS. PLUM	Wireless internet *please.*
ARTHUR	Wireless internet please.
MOLL	The roots have torn up the cabling. You'll have to do it the old-fashioned way.
ARTHUR	What does that mean?
MOLL	Magazines.

MOLL and ARTHUR smile.

MRS. PLUM	They were still doing the square when we got married, I remember because we'd planned to go through there on the way back from the service but there was all sorts of rubble and tractors and things. Do you remember Clive?

MR. PLUM	That's right.
MRS. PLUM	It was a very nice wedding indeed, I have to say. Very tastefully done. David Scott from interflora did the decorations for us. Sweet peas, 'Show Girl' peonies, spray roses and lavender. Then senecio, rosemary and peppercorns too on the tables. It was lovely.
MANZ	There's lights coming from the square. People are gathering. Looters, I think.
HARDY	Let's go.
MOLL	Don't. Wait here. Ocados will come. You'll see.
MANZ	We won't risk more than half an hour. We'll be careful.
HARDY	If we don't go now everything will be snatched.
MOLL	I'm sure Ocados will come.
HARDY	Moll, it's alright.
	He takes a gun from his bag.
MOLL	Where did you get that?
ARTHUR	Wow.
HARDY	I thought I might need it.
MOLL	Why?
HARDY	To shoot something. Look, if we don't get food soon, we'll starve, or be too weak to stand a chance.
MOLL	But –
HARDY	Moll.
ARTHUR	Can I come?
	They look at him.

25

ARTHUR	I want to use the gun.
HARDY	No.
ARTHUR	I can be brave. Tell him, Dad.
MANZ	You stay here. We need some of our best people here, to protect Moll.
MR. PLUM	I should go with the boys.
MRS. PLUM	No, Clive, you stay. There's no point in everyone going.
MANZ	I can hear people shouting.
MR. PLUM	Perhaps you're right. We'll hold the fort here.
MRS. PLUM	Exactly. Stay here with Arthur, that's your job. We'll stay here for Arthur.
HARDY	Come on.

They leave.

ii)

ARTHUR and MOLL are in the room alone.

MOLL is dozing. ARTHUR is climbing in the branches of the tree.

MOLL wakes.

MOLL takes out a cigarette and lights it. She smokes.

The sound of rustling stops. Suddenly, he swings, upside down, hanging by his knees, looking at the old woman.

He stares at the cigarette.

MOLL	Where are your parents?
ARTHUR	Having a bath.
MOLL	They went home? How?

26

ARTHUR No.

MOLL They're having a bath here?

ARTHUR shrugs, upside down. MOLL shivers.

ARTHUR Can I nick a fag?

MOLL You're a bit young to smoke.

ARTHUR I'm not that young. I just look young to you because you're so old.

MOLL How old are you?

ARTHUR Eleven. *(She moves the cigarette away.)* And a half.

Pause.

She holds the cigarette forward. He swings down and eagerly takes it from her.

He begins to smoke.

She takes out another cigarette and lights up.

MOLL Well?

ARTHUR Thank you.

They sit together, smoking. At length they finish.

ARTHUR Shall we twos another?

She takes out another and lights it.

She passes it to ARTHUR.

ARTHUR Thank you.

They pass it between each other, taking a few drags at a time.

ARTHUR You've not got anything harder? Any weed? Skunk? Any coke?

MOLL I've got some smack in the fridge.

ARTHUR	Really?
MOLL	No. I have Yakult, it's the only thing left. Will that do?
	ARTHUR goes to get the Yakult.
ARTHUR	Do you want one?
MOLL	Yes.
ARTHUR	Who are those boys?
MOLL	They look after me.
ARTHUR	Why?
MOLL	Obligation.
ARTHUR	What does that mean?
MOLL	Guilt.
ARTHUR	Are they your sons?
MOLL	No.
ARTHUR	Are they your toy boys?
MOLL	No.
ARTHUR	Do you love them?
MOLL	No.
ARTHUR	Do you love anyone?
MOLL	Yes.
ARTHUR	Who?
MOLL	Myself.
ARTHUR	Have you ever been in love with someone not including yourself?
MOLL	Of course.

ARTHUR	Who?
MOLL	Paul Newman.
ARTHUR	Who's that?
MOLL	Another knight.
ARTHUR	Are you married?
MOLL	Not any more.
ARTHUR	When were you married?
MOLL	Never. I just said not any more to make sure you didn't feel sorry for me.
ARTHUR	Have you been in love though yeah?
MOLL	Yes. Everyone's been in love.
ARTHUR	In the war?

Pause.

I remember the first time I fell in love. It was in Campbell Park, down by the canal. They'd boarded up the adventure playground because it wasn't safe. Me and Cal were hitting up the boards on the canal side, where no one's around. I got bored so me and Cal walked round the park a bit. Nicole Clark was standing, leaning against the railings of the running track. I knew her because she used to go to my school, but she left last year to go to secondary. She's one of the most beautiful girls in the world, with massive tits and a really pretty face. We went up to her and Cal asked her for a cigarette. She laughed at Cal's face and I started laughing too. Cal got all annoyed and stormed off, calling me names. I stayed standing next to Nicole though and we just stood there in silence. It was dead pretty. I looked at her and touched her leg. Like this. She's a bit taller than me, because she's older, but I just stood there touching her leg. It was really nice and really warm and I just stood there, falling in love. She didn't look at me, so I began to feel up her leg. I could feel her pants, soft like a cushion, and when I put my fingers inside her pants I could feel her hair, which was a bit of a surprise. That's when I knew I was in love. It was like a song or something, when you feel your heart go. I started to finger her a bit, just stick two fingers in and out, but my arm hurt from holding it upright so I stopped. It's the best feeling in the world, love.

MOLL   Yes. That sounds very nice. Love can be a beautiful thing.

ARTHUR   The adventure playground's not there anymore. It's just park. The train tracks too. Are you sure you're not in love with those boys? Do you think they can get some weed for me?

MOLL   Plants are dangerous.

ARTHUR   When they come back I'll ask them if they can get some weed for me.

MOLL   What's going on out there?

ARTHUR runs to the window but can't see out. He drags a chair over, climbs onto the chair, and from there onto the kitchen surface. He looks out of the window.

ARTHUR   It's night. There are lights though, from machines I think. Looks like some machines

30

have come in. I can't see much. There are some soldiers or firemen or something talking in Tesco pointing at the trees. I think they're trying to chop them down. There's a soldier with a chainsaw trying to clear the door to Vision Express.

MOLL   Are the boys down there?

ARTHUR   Which boys?

MOLL   The boys that were here before? Are they down there?

ARTHUR   Didn't I just say, I could only see machines and soldiers and all the trees. Can I have another Yakult?

MOLL   Yes.

ARTHUR   I like your hair. It's like silver.

MOLL   Thank you. I like yours. It's like gold.

ARTHUR   Who's King Arthur?

MOLL   He was a king who lived a very long time ago. When England was all covered in woods and forests. He had a lot of knights who fought for him and a wife called Guinevere.

ARTHUR   Was she buff?

MOLL   Yes. He had a sword like that one that he pulled from a stone, which is how people knew he was king.

ARTHUR   I got this at Toys 'R' Us. I put it in my school bag and walked out.

MOLL   They didn't have Toys 'R' Us then. His sword was better than yours anyway.

ARTHUR	Did you know him?
MOLL	Not personally.
ARTHUR	What was Guinevere like?
MOLL	Gentle and kind.
ARTHUR	Blonde?
MOLL	I don't know.
ARTHUR	Probably blonde. What did they do, the knights?
MOLL	They fought and ate and rode horses round the forests.
ARTHUR	Cool.
MOLL	Do you have any knights?
ARTHUR	I had Cal. But he left in class six because his dad works in Coventry.
MOLL	Poor thing.
	Silence.
ARTHUR	Are the boys your knights?
MOLL	Sometimes. I don't really have any either.
ARTHUR	What does Moll mean?
MOLL	Nothing. It just sounds nice.
ARTHUR	I like it.
MOLL	Yes. It's not a real name though, like Arthur. That's a real name.
	Pause.
ARTHUR	I'm hungry.
MOLL	Me too.

ARTHUR   I wish I could have gone down with the boys,
              with the gun. I would have got you something
              to eat.

              Silence.

              *There's a turn in the lock and the door opens. HARDY
              and MANZ enter.*

              MR. and MRS. PLUM come in wearing towels.

MR. PLUM   Here we go.

MRS. PLUM   At last!

MOLL   What took so long? Did you find anything?

              The boys look defeated.

              Did you loot anything for me?

HARDY   It's all gone. All been taken.

MRS. PLUM   What about Nandos? Did you try Nandos?

MANZ   Stripped. There's nothing left.

MR. PLUM   What are we going to do?

MRS. PLUM   Don't be greedy, Clive. I'm sure they did their
              best.

MOLL   Did you manage anything?

              *MANZ reveals a mangled Boots bag and hands it to
              MOLL.*

              *She takes from it a lipsalve stick, some paracetemol,
              another lipsalve stick, and a third lipsalve stick.*

MANZ   Sorry.

HARDY   It's chaos down there. When we came out
              into the square it was like being in a forest.
              Underneath our feet the stones, the old paving

stones have been ripped up. There were lights from somewhere, and they'd already tried getting the machines close enough to do some damage, but nothing was working. We managed to find our way to Wagamama. Branches had smashed through the windows, and in the restaurant the floor had been ripped up by cotton grass and pond sedge. Someone had looted a gas cylinder from the kitchen and was trying to get it lit, trying to burn down the wood, but it wouldn't catch. We skirted round the square, keeping to the outside. The middle was so dark, just shadows of looters, and howls of people lost in there. Bonfires were springing up round the outside, people piling the paper and folders out of Rymans and burning them up, trying to make it catch the edge of the forest, but it's not working. Nothing's working. Eventually we found Tescos, but it had all gone. A couple of rotten ready meals left on the till, an empty can of Lilt in the fridge. Apart from that: nothing. Cleaned out. The floor was smeared with smashed pasta sauces and microwave shepherd's pies, dotted with footprints from jackboots and deer. We got to Boots, but it wasn't much better. We took what we could.

They look at the lipsalves. Pause.

ARTHUR   Did you go to Game?

HARDY   Eh?

ARTHUR   Did you go past Game at all?

HARDY   On Hills Road? That's ten minutes away.

ARTHUR	It's just, I thought you might have picked me something up. *(He holds up his PSP.)*
	There's a scratching on the door.
MOLL	Ocados?
	She goes to open the door.
HARDY	Careful.
	She looks through the peeper.
MOLL	It's Winston!
HARDY	Don't open the door.
MOLL	What do you mean? It's Winston.
HARDY	You didn't see it down there. They're not scared of us any more. You don't know who he's with.
MOLL	I can see, look he's on his… *(She fades out to silence.)*
MANZ	What?
MOLL	There's another cat with him. A ginger Tom.
HARDY	Moll. Do not open that door.
MOLL	They're both there, looking at the door. Winston's looking at me. I want to let him in.
MRS. PLUM	Please don't open the door. I'm afraid. And Clive is allergic to cats.
MR. PLUM	It's not bad, but they do irritate my skin.
MOLL	Winston! There's more, four of them now. They're all there, lying outside the door. And another, coming down the stairs. A big tabby. They're looking at me.
MANZ	We can't let them in, Moll.

MOLL	He's my cat.
HARDY	Not any more.
MOLL	Winston.

3.

i)

A dense wood. The next day. All that remains of the flat is MOLL's chair.

MANZ, MOLL, ARTHUR and his PARENTS are there, famished and weak. HARDY is elsewhere.

MRS. PLUM is holding WINSTON's tin of catfood. It's now empty. She runs her finger along the inside and sucks it. There's nothing left.

MANZ	Do you know how to build a fire?
ARTHUR	I'm hungry.
MANZ	This will take your mind off it. Have you made a fire before?
ARTHUR	Me and Cal once made flame throwers from his step-brother's Lynx.
MANZ	The important thing is to make sure you've got all the big bits at the bottom and then the smaller bits, the twigs, on the top, in a wigwam. There.
ARTHUR	I'm hungry.
MR. PLUM	I'm sure Hardy will be back soon.
ARTHUR	What will he bring?
MR. PLUM	Whatever he can catch.
ARTHUR	I hope he brings Subway.
MANZ	Where are the matches?
MR. PLUM	We had two packs… Here. Ah! Ants. The box is filled with ants.
MANZ	And the matches?
MR. PLUM	Gone.

MANZ	Where's the other box?
	They scurry to look for the box.
ARTHUR	Here!
	They huddle round the box. He's about to open it.
MR. PLUM	Let Manz do it darling.
	ARTHUR hands it to MANZ.
	Slowly, he pokes the matchbox open.
	They breathe a sigh of relief.

ii)

The same, later. Still no fire.

ARTHUR	Are you hungry?
MOLL	Yes. Are you?
ARTHUR	Yes. But I'm trying to be brave.
	He picks up a leaf from the ground. He tries to bite into it, but it's too tough.
	MANZ is trying to get the fire going with a packet of matches.
MOLL	Don't waste them. You're wasting them. Wait till Hardy gets back, he'll do it.
MANZ	I can do it.
MOLL	You're not having much luck.
ARTHUR	Mum, I'm hungry.
MANZ	Fuck! Fucking stupid, shit matches. Fucking fire.
ARTHUR	Dad! When will he be here?
MRS. PLUM	Try again Clive.

MR. PLUM	Why? What's the point? There's no signal. The canopy's blocking it out. Or birds have got to the lines and pecked them out.
MRS. PLUM	What's the harm in trying?

MR. PLUM takes his phone and holds it up, looking for signal. He follows it round, like a gold prospector, holding it up and down. He searches around the copse.

MR. PLUM	Happy?

iii)

They all sit. They are almost drunk with hunger.

The fire has been scattered, unlit, as if kicked apart.

MANZ is fuming, pacing around.

MRS. PLUM	I tell you what's amazing. That someone actually *invented* ovens. Do you see what I mean? Once there weren't ovens. Then there were. Someone must have invented them. Mr. Oven? Or Mrs. Oven.
ARTHUR	What did they eat before that?
MRS. PLUM	Good question, darling. Raw food I suppose.
ARTHUR	Sushi?
MR. PLUM	Sandwiches.
MRS. PLUM	Chocolate.

There is a rustling offstage.

MOLL	Hardy?
MANZ	Careful Moll, it might be an animal.

The rustling gets nearer.

HARDY enters, ragged and battered.

HARDY   I did it.

MRS. PLUM Well done!

MR. PLUM   Very well done!

MOLL   Where is it? What did you kill?

HARDY   Here.

He takes out a dead hedgehog from his bag.

Pause.

HARDY   It fought like a cunt, but I got him in the end.
               Broke his neck.

Pause.

HARDY   I tracked it to its burrow. I looked for its prints
               in the dirt then followed them.

MR. PLUM   The prickles must have stung a lot when you
               grabbed it.

HARDY   They did actually.

Silence.

MRS. PLUM Do you think there were any more where this
               one came from?

HARDY   It's a start isn't it?

MRS. PLUM Oh yes. A very good start.

MR. PLUM   Very good.

HARDY   Let's cook it then. Where's the fire?

MOLL   There was some trouble getting it lit.

MANZ   There's no fuel, no paper or anything. The
               wood won't catch. The leaves just make smoke.

40

HARDY	This whole time you couldn't get a fire started?
MANZ	It's impossible. It won't catch. We'll just have to enjoy this *feast* raw.
HARDY	Is there something wrong with my hedgehog?
MANZ	It's not going to go very far.
HARDY	It's a start.
MANZ	It's a starter. It's fun-sized. It's a happy meal. You've got a *gun*, I thought you'd at least bring back a rabbit or something, a bird. The amount of time you took we were holding out for a deer.
HARDY	I hunted.
MANZ	I'll hunt. I can hunt. I'll do better than *this*.
HARDY	Yeah of course you will you weed. What were you doing when I've been out getting this? You think this was easy? I had to *hound* this. I *tracked* it down. I crawled through bushes and shrubs and up trees and into trenches and swum though rivers. I got it. I *provided* it.
MANZ	It's a fucking hedgehog! What are we going to do with a hedgehog between six of us? You're a real commando. A real fucking Rambo.
HARDY	Yeah I am, yeah I am. I am a fucking commando. I *killed* this hedgehog. I *killed* it so Moll could eat. I found its shitty little hole and I reached my arm into it and it bit me and squealed at me but I pulled it out and snapped its little neck so Moll could eat!
MANZ	If we don't find something proper to eat we're going to starve. You were supposed to keep

us alive. We need a meal, not a fucking *amuse-bouche*. We need an animal!

There is a rustling sound from offstage.

Enter OCADO MAN.

The OCADO MAN stands upstage centre. He is bedraggled, his uniform is torn to shreds and he is shell-shocked. In his hands are colour-coded plastic bags.

They stare at him.

MOLL   It's Ocados!

OCADO MAN   Miss Crane?

MOLL   Yes.

OCADO MAN   Good.

   They run to him and grab the bags, desperately looking for anything they can get out of them. They're empty.

I was attacked. My van was useless, stuck in a bog, stuck in Parson's Road. I left it there you see. I set out on foot. I got told, Mr. Sanderson told me, another complaint from a customer, another missed order, and I was liable to get the sack. To get fired. He said he'd hook me if it happened again. I didn't want to risk it. It's the whole company that's at stake, that's what Sanderson says. I'm a representative of the whole company, so I'm not to let them down. It's actually quite a responsibility when you think of it. I'm an ambassador. So it's up to me to provide the goods, to get them to the address. Well, that's why I set out on foot. It was alright at first. Headed down Alders Way,

42

towards the Corn Exchange. I'd planned to
nip round the back of the Odeon and come
at you that way. I'd say it was almost pretty.
Quite idyllic actually. There's no road anymore,
but it's not like this yet. There's little saplings,
bushes and reeds. The edge of Copling Street's
fallen in and got filled in with rain water.
There's all sorts there now, it's like a stream,
trickling down the hill. Frogs, toads, beavers,
fish. Dragonflies as big as my finger. And the
birds! Ducks and geese and swans everywhere.
Others that I don't know the names of, great
big ones overhead, little ones twitching their
heads at me. I stopped and had a paddle. That's
where I lost my shoes. A little fox came and
nicked them when I was paddling. So I pushed
off from the pond barefoot. Still had all the bags
at this point: fridge, cupboard,

MOLL   Freezer.

OCADO MAN   Yes, freezer. Packed full. Oh, the stuff I had
for you in those bags. I mean, you'll know, you
ordered it but, oh the glory! Oh lord! There
was cooked hams and cured meats, diced
chicken and ready-to-eat veg. I had olives for
the oldies, and Fabs for the little ones. Crisps
and chocolate and cereals and coffee. In the
cupboard bag, I had a plastic box full of mini
doughnuts. Each one was like a perfect wheel,
dusted with icing sugar, delicate as snow. I
tasted one. I know I shouldn't have but I got so
hungry on the journey. I tasted one and – oh
– it was soft, so soft, and the sugar fell into my
mouth as if the very air had been sweetened.

I let the dough dissolve in my mouth, I let
my saliva sit with it, let it soak until I had to
swallow the whole thing down.

They got me outside Habitat. It was forest by
that point. So dark and dense, like this. There
was barely anything left of the shop, but I could
see the remains of sofas, stuck in the branches
of a birch. An armchair, right up high, with a
warbling robin nesting in its back. They ripped
the food from the bags, even the frozen stuff.
They knocked me to the ground and kicked
and bit and scratched me. I tried to hold on. I
thought about what Mr. Sanderson would say
when I got back to the depot. I knew it was the
end, he'd throw me out on my ear. But they
were too strong, too many. They ate in front
of my face. They gobbled it down like wolves.
They crammed the fruit and veg into their
hungry mouths. They tore open the bagels and
the pitta bread and ate them in two bites. They
moaned and growled in ecstasy. And they fed
their young with the crisps and the raw meat.
The milk ran down their throats and down their
necks in great rivers, sticky and thick. Crème
fraiche, pork pies, oven pizzas, gone. And when
they had finished, when there was not so much
as a puff of dusty sugar left in the air, they left
me, face down in the earth, my wrist sprained,
my nose bloodied. I didn't know what else to
do, so I went on. And I did it. I made it here.
And I saved something. I did manage to save
something.

Slowly, he removes from under his shirt… a microwave chicken jalfrezi.

He holds it out to MOLL.

Slowly, MANZ, takes it from the OCADO MAN and presents it to MOLL.

Tenderly, quietly, MOLL removes the paper sleeve and the plastic top. She looks around for a fork or a knife but knows there isn't one there to find. She rolls up her sleeve and delicate as if she were stitching lace, begins to eat the ready meal with her hands. The others gather round and she feeds them too, allowing them to dip their hands in and take rice and chicken and gravy.

At length, they're done.

HARDY   It's not enough.

The OCADO MAN collapses to his knees and stares outwards.

Silence.

They all look at him.

Silence.

MR. PLUM   He'll be fired if he does ever make it back.

Pause.

MRS. PLUM   Clive's right, he'll be out on his ear, that's what he said.

MR. PLUM   He'd be finished.

Pause.

HARDY   Unless we have a fire, it doesn't matter.

MANZ   I'll get the fire going. I will, I'll get it going.

MR. PLUM   We'll all help. Arthur'll get brushwood, won't you Arthur?

He nods.

Pause.

HARDY   He'll never make it back.

MRS. PLUM   Someone'll have him if we won't.

MANZ   He's barely got a breath in him anyway.

Pause. MOLL is apart sitting by a tree. The others are either side of OCADO MAN. They all look at each other. They're in agreement.

They look to MOLL.

Pause.

MOLL   He'd be out on his ear.

Pause. They approach the OCADO MAN. Now swaying on his knees with exhaustion.

They have him surrounded, all standing above him in an open circle.

Pause.

They look at each other.

MRS. PLUM   Well…

HARDY   Right…

Pause.

MANZ, feebly raises his arm to strike. He gives the OCADO MAN a little hit on the head.

OCADO MAN   Ow.

MRS. PLUM   Come on!

MANZ   What do you mean come on?!

HARDY   Look, we need a – a rock or something.

They scatter to try to find a rock.

MR. PLUM   There's nothing here.

MRS. PLUM   It's just leaves and grass.

The OCADO MAN is wobbling to his feet. He tries to leave, but flops to his knees again.

MRS. PLUM   Come on!

HARDY   I'm thinking!

MANZ strides back up to OCADO MAN, with determination. He takes a deep breath, raises his hand to strike, swipes, but at the last minute checks himself and ends up just rapping him on the head again.

OCADO MAN   Ow. Please stop doing that.

HARDY   Shut up. Just shut up, I'm trying to think. The bags! The shopping bags!

He grabs one of the Ocado bags and wraps it around his fists, pulling it taut.

He approaches the OCADO MAN and attempts to strangle him. It works a bit, but soon, the bag rips.

HARDY   Arrrgh.

MANZ   Arrrrgh! *(He approaches the man again, really tries to gee himself up to do it, but again just ends up hitting him quite lightly on the head.)* Fucking hell!

MR. PLUM   Look. Look. He's nearly gone. He's not far now. Let's just wait. Sit it out and soon he'll do it all by himself.

They look around. No one's got any better ideas.

They all go to the bases of various trees and sit and wait.

47

	A long silence.
MOLL	So how's it going?
MANZ	He's a survivor.
MOLL	Right. So what's the plan?
HARDY	We're waiting it out.
MOLL	Ah. How noble.
MANZ	It's more dignified.
HARDY	For him.
MANZ	Yes. Well, and for us.
	Silence.
MOLL	And has there been any progress?
	OCADO MAN gives a little cough.
MANZ	Some.
	Silence.
MRS. PLUM	Ahem. Maybe we should play a game to pass the time?
HARDY	I really don't think that's…
MANZ	It doesn't feel quite…
	Silence.
	The OCADO MAN stumbles to his feet. The group watch. He stumbles slowly towards where he came from.
MRS. PLUM	He's getting away!
	ARTHUR stands up. He is holding Hardy's gun. He picks up a large branch from the would-be fire and approaches the OCADO MAN from behind. He uses the branch to swipe the OCADO MAN's legs from beneath him. The

48

OCADO MAN collapses and ARTHUR shoots him in the head three times.

Pause.

ARTHUR   There.

MRS. PLUM   Well done darling. Well done.

Silence.

iv)

The wood, later. There is blood on their hands and clothes.

HARDY is staring at his hands.

A sound offstage.

MRS. PLUM   What's that?

A sound offstage.

MRS. PLUM   What is it Clive?

MR. PLUM   I don't know Mary, do I?

A third sound.

MRS. PLUM   I can't stay here.

MR. PLUM   Where would you like to go?

MRS. PLUM   Where's Tim? Let's try to find Tim.

MR. PLUM   Mary.

MRS. PLUM   Arthur. Come here. It's time to go on another adventure now alright. Mummy and Daddy want to go on another adventure.

ARTHUR   Where to?

MRS. PLUM   To find Uncle Tim. Won't that be nice?

MR. PLUM	That's right. We might go to find Uncle Tim. He's a bit of a journey away though, that's all. So we might have to go on a bit of a journey to find him.
ARTHUR	Is Moll coming with us?
MRS. PLUM	Moll has to stay here. This is where she lives.
ARTHUR	This is where we live too, now.
MANZ	It's a bear.
MRS. PLUM	A bear!
MANZ	The smell of the meat. It's attracting animals.
HARDY	No.
MANZ	It won't come into the camp yet, the noise will make it suspicious.
HARDY	It's just a matter of time.
MR. PLUM	Since when did we have bears in England?
MANZ	About a week ago I read there was a sighting at Plymouth. I didn't think they'd get this far north this quickly.
MRS. PLUM	There it is again!
ARTHUR	I'll kill it.
MRS. PLUM	No darling.
ARTHUR	Yes I will I'll have it. Lend me the gun again, I'll do it in.
MANZ	This one's a job for grown-ups. Stay here. Hardy and I'll go.
HARDY	OK.
MANZ	Come on Hardy. Let's go.

MR. PLUM	Why does anyone have to go? There'll be more after that one anyway. Can't we try and escape? Head north and try to outrun the seeds.
HARDY	There's no chance of that. It's spread too quickly.
MANZ	Besides…
MR. PLUM	Yes?
MRS. PLUM	What is it?
	Pause.
HARDY	Tell them.
MANZ	This morning. After. When you were all still sleeping. Hardy and I tried to forage for something to eat. We couldn't pull up any of the plants, all the leaves were too tough but we were desperate. So we kept looking. We must have gone almost a mile north when we saw it. They've built a wall. A plastic wall as high as the canopy. Redwoods, oaks and pines are pressed to it, their roots are crunching against it. The army must have encircled us. Given up the South and tried to stop the seed spreading any further.
MR. PLUM	Well that's good news. There must be a door, a checkpoint somewhere?
HARDY	There is.
MR. PLUM	So? Let's go.
	Pause.
MR. PLUM	Well?
HARDY	They won't have the boy. And they won't have Moll.

51

MANZ	To get through the checkpoint you have to be decontaminated. But it's heavy stuff. They won't do it to any one they think is…frail.
MRS. PLUM	Of course they will.
HARDY	There were dozens of children there. Abandoned the wrong side of the wall. They won't let them through.
MRS. PLUM	No.
MR. PLUM	That sound again. It's getting closer.

Pause.

MANZ	Let's go. Hardy?
HARDY	We have to.
MANZ	Clive?
MR. PLUM	Yes. Alright.
MRS. PLUM	Oh Clive.

They make to leave.

MOLL	Won't you need the gun?

They stop. They go to take it from her.

MOLL	Good luck.

They go.

A long silence. MOLL and ARTHUR sit together.

MRS. PLUM watches them.

MOLL	When Hardy was a little boy he used to sit by the window and kill flies. Smudge them into the glass. Manz would sit and watch him. Hours and hours. They must have got through a hundred flies a day at their peak. They'll be alright.

Another long silence.

ARTHUR   Do you know what this is?

He takes the green Ocado bag and floats it through the air.

MOLL   No. What is it?

ARTHUR   A dragon.

MOLL smiles.

MOLL   Once upon a time there were two dragons sitting together in the forest. Suddenly a knight in shining armour came walking into the glade. The first dragon looked at his mate and said, 'Breakfast!'. The second replied 'Nah, I don't feel like canned food'.

They smile. MRS. PLUM smiles.

MR. PLUM re-enters.

MR PLUM: They did it.

ARTHUR   They killed the bear?

MR. PLUM   Yes darling, they killed the bear.

ARTHUR   How?

MR. PLUM   They approached it from behind. It was asleep.

ARTHUR   Why was it making so much noise then? Are you sure it was the right bear?

MR. PLUM   It was tired from making all the noise. It was the right bear. It woke up anyway, made a noise. The same noise.

ARTHUR   Was it big?

MR. PLUM   As big as Mum's Astra. It stood up on its back legs. It roared. Hardy shot it.

ARTHUR   Where?

MR. PLUM   Here. Through the neck. It fell on the ground and the tree shook.

ARTHUR   Where was it?

MR. PLUM   Just near here. It was coming for the man. We got it just in time.

ARTHUR   Why didn't we hear the gun?

MR. PLUM   It had a silencer on. It was ever so quiet. Hardy didn't want to disturb the other animals and attract attention. He was very brave. Very brave.

ARTHUR   Are they bringing the bear back? Will we eat it?

MR. PLUM   No. It's too heavy.

ARTHUR   So shall we go and eat it there?

MR. PLUM   We can't eat it. It was poisoned. From the berries it was eating.

ARTHUR   Where are the boys?

MR. PLUM   With the bear. Making sure it's dead.

ARTHUR   Why didn't they come back with you?

MR. PLUM   They wanted to make sure the bear was dead. So you were safe. Look, they'll be back soon with bear steaks. They're going to cut off some big juicy bear steaks and bring them back here for breakfast.

MRS. PLUM   Won't that be nice?

ARTHUR   But won't they be poisoned?

MR. PLUM   They'll be careful to cut only from the clean side. So if you have a rest, get some sleep, and

	then before you know it, it will be time for the best breakfast you've ever had.
ARTHUR	OK. I want to sleep over here with Moll. Moll, why are you crying?
MRS. PLUM	She's very proud of her boys.
ARTHUR	Me too.

ARTHUR goes over to lie by MOLL.

MR. PLUM looks at MRS. PLUM.

He makes an incomprehensible signal with his eyes.

She doesn't understand.

He tries again, it's even more incomprehensible.

She still doesn't understand.

He tries again.

She understands.

They look at ARTHUR, lying on MOLL.

Silence.

MRS. PLUM goes to ARTHUR.

MRS. PLUM Sweet dreams, Arthur. Sweet dreams.

Blackout.

v)

The wood, the next morning. Only MOLL and ARTHUR are there.

MOLL is awake, ARTHUR is asleep in her lap.

Silence.

MOLL Got it. Ahem.

What's the difference between a hen night and a trip to the zoo?

Well one's full of loud, hairy animals being poked in public by men in uniform.

And the other has a gift shop.

ARTHUR wakes up.

He looks around. They are alone. MR. and MRS. PLUM are nowhere to be seen.

ARTHUR looks behind a tree. He returns to the camp.

Pause.

He goes to another tree and looks around there too, before returning to camp.

Silence.

ARTHUR   Tell me about King Arthur again.

MOLL   I don't know very much.

ARTHUR   Was he strong?

MOLL   I expect so.

ARTHUR   And brave?

MOLL   Yes. He was very brave.

ARTHUR   Did he kill and stab people he didn't like.

MOLL   No. He was very generous. Even his best friend, who betrayed him and stole his wife.

ARTHUR   Gingerbeer?

MOLL   Yes, Gingerbeer. He didn't even kill him.

ARTHUR   When was that? The Second World War?

MOLL	No, before that. When England still had lions and dragons and fairy tale princesses. When ghosts rustled in the trees. There weren't streets. There weren't shops. Just copses and brooks and clearings and dells.
ARTHUR	And castles?
MOLL	Big castles by the sea or on hills.

From offstage there is the sound of frenzied whooping and shouting. It is the sound of children. Tens, maybe hundreds of children, careering through the forest, wild and war-like.

ARTHUR rushes to the edge of the clearing to see. He places himself between the sound and MOLL.

ARTHUR	Children.
MOLL	Must be hundreds of them.
ARTHUR	Laughing.
MOLL	Going to attack the wall?
ARTHUR	Wicked.

ARTHUR takes a step towards the forest. Then stops.

MOLL	Why aren't you running?
ARTHUR	I can't.
MOLL	Why?
ARTHUR	I have to stay here.
MOLL	Why?
ARTHUR	In case anything happens. I have to stay here in case.

Another whooping group of children pass.

MOLL and ARTHUR listen to the sounds disappear into the distance.

Silence.

MOLL   Thank you.

ARTHUR   Do you think Nicole Clark is on this side of the wall? I hope she got through.

MOLL is looking in her handbag. She takes out her blusher.

Why are you still putting on your make-up?

MOLL   To look beautiful.

ARTHUR   I think you are beautiful. For a grandma.

MOLL   Thank you.

ARTHUR kisses her on the lips.

MOLL   You should have gone with the kids.

ARTHUR   Your face feels loose. Loose and dry.

MOLL takes from her bag one of the lispalves that were looted earlier and applies it.

They kiss again.

ARTHUR   That's a bit better.

MOLL   Thank you.

ARTHUR   You're not as good a kisser as Shadima from class six.

MOLL gets out her cigarettes.

MOLL   Last one.

ARTHUR   Shall we twos it?

MOLL   Yes.

She puts it in her mouth and then realises she has nothing to light it with.

The boy gets up, roots around the dead fire and finds the box of matches.

ARTHUR There's one left.

MOLL Yes.

Carefully, he strikes the match and, with it, the cigarette. They watch the match burn to the end, and he throws it away.

They smoke.

There is a sound from offstage. A rustling of leaves.

The BRIDE enters. She is dressed in a pink T-shirt which enhances her cleavage, and a miniskirt. On the back of the T-Shirt reads 'The Bride'. She is wearing a cheap plastic crown. She is clutching a piece of paper in her hand.

ARTHUR Moll, look. There *are* still princesses in the forest. She's got the most beautiful tits I've ever seen. She looks like a porn star!

MOLL She's not a real princess.

ARTHUR Yes she is. A real princess. She's like all my dreams have come true. I bet she's easy. I bet she's gagging for it, Moll. Is *this* what love is?

MOLL Yes.

ARTHUR Are you jealous Moll? Are you jealous because she's so young and I don't fancy you?

MOLL Yes.

ARTHUR But you're not interested in sex are you Moll? Not any more. Not like her. Look at her skirt.

MOLL	It's a very nice skirt.
ARTHUR	You are a real princess aren't you?

The BRIDE opens her mouth to speak, but nothing comes out. She tries again, but nothing comes again.

The piece of paper drops from her hand. ARTHUR picks it up and hands it to MOLL.

MOLL *(Reading.)* 'I'm getting married tomorrow! Before I get hitched I must complete six tasks: One. Snog a bald man.

The BRIDE nods.

Two. Get a man's pants.

The BRIDE holds up some men's pants. They have blood on them.

Three. Swap an item of clothing with a man.

She holds up a bloody shirt.

Get a man to flash his bum at me.

She nods, and cries.

Enjoy one last kiss of freedom: snog the sexiest guy in the club.

She looks at the ARTHUR, collecting herself. She goes to him and kisses him slowly on the lips.

Last one. Enjoy one last dance of freedom: slow dance with the sexiest guy in the club.'

She takes out her phone and begins to play some music.

She looks at ARTHUR. He holds her by the waist and they dance, slowly and romantically.

Music surges.

ARTHUR lets go of the bride and turns to face MOLL. He approaches her and holds her waist. They begin to dance.

The bride picks up the discarded list of tasks. She looks at them, then looks out.

BRIDE   Mum, Dad, Alex, Kate, and everyone who's come tonight. I want to first thank Mum so much for organising this evening. And Dad for paying for it. But most of all I want to thank you, Scott. Thank you for being the love of my life. Thank you for making your vows to me and for allowing me to make mine to you. We will wake up tomorrow next to each other and our lives will never be the same. I want to be with you for the rest of my life. And I can't wait. The world seems fresh, full and alive. Birds are singing, the sun is shining. And we have a whole new future ahead of us.

Music continues.

Curtain.

I'M NOT HERE RIGHT NOW

I'm Not Here Right Now was first performed at the Paines Plough Roundabout on 7th August 2015 in a co-production with Soho Theatre and featured the following cast and creative team:

THE NARRATOR   Thomas Eccleshare
CLARE   Valentina Ceschi

Directed by   Steve Marmion
Lighting by   Amy Mae
Music and Sound by   Tom Mills

Characters

CLARE

THE NARRATOR

A note on the text

The Narrator's text is important to stick to, because it carries
the narrative in a specific way. However, if you feel the show
could be better served with different actions from Clare, or
with multiple bodies as Clare, or with a puppet as Clare,
then ignore the stage directions as written. The directions
in this text were a starting point for rehearsals but it was my
intention that Clare's actions would grow to become another
part of the writing; juxtaposing, contradicting or confirming
the Narrator at different points. The crucial thing is that there
is at least some relationship between the descriptions the
Narrator is giving and the physical 'reality' on stage.

A slice of an apartment.

A coffee table, on which are some magazines and scientific journals, a book or two, some sheets of notepaper and a mobile phone. A chair. On the floor is a full, serious-looking backpack.

[note: There should be at least some <u>real</u> elements of the flat; some things, like a table or a chair, which are undoubtedly the objects being described.]

Also in the room, but perhaps unseen, are a window looking out onto a busy street, a front door onto a corridor and a route to the kitchen, bathroom and bedroom.

Elsewhere, separate from the apartment set, is a plain desk with a neat pile of printed paper.

The NARRATOR enters, looks carefully at the apartment, acknowledges the audience, then sits at the desk. He begins to read from the pile of paper.

THE NARRATOR   A room in a small apartment.

A table, a chair, some magazines and papers.

A door to a bathroom off to one side.

A toilet flushes.

(To an audience member.) That's you I'm afraid. Yeah you're sitting in the toilet. *(To someone else.)* You're in the bath.

It's evening, about 6:30, and if you were to look out of the window of the apartment you would see the evening sky turning into night.

The muffled sound of traffic and passers-by a couple of floors below.

The sounds of the road outside drift in. Passers-by. Cars. A cyclist swearing at the cars.

The sound of water running from the bathroom.

A mobile phone on the table begins to vibrate.

A mobile phone begins to vibrate.

Then stops.

Then stops.

The tap stops running.

In the apartment lives a thirty year old woman.

A woman enters the apartment. The NARRATOR watches her for a beat.

Her name is Clare Sahakian.

She checks her phone, seeing that there are unheard messages, and places it back down.

CLARE picks up the phone, checks it, and puts it down.

She sits down on the chair.

CLARE sits. The NARRATOR watches her. He allows a moment of possibility.

Clare is a research scientist at Cambridge University. She was born in Slovenia in 1984, in a small town called Bovec, on the border of the Triglavski national park. Her father worked for the forestry department, trying to stem the illegal logging that was taking place throughout the park.

Clare has had a long day. She's just got back to the flat and doesn't want to think about anything. She goes to the kitchen, opens a bottle of wine, pours herself a glass and returns to the sofa with both.

CLARE goes offstage and returns with the an opened bottle of wine and a glass.

She takes the weight off her feet.

CLARE puts her feet up.

And takes a sip.

CLARE takes a sip.

When she was growing up she would follow her dad out to the park and roam around the woods; tramping through the parkland, kicking up leaves, or climbing up through the branches of the huge oaks, checking the wire traps for signs of poachers or, in the nineties once she was a teenager, checking the power supply to the CCTV cameras.

Clare takes a long sip from her glass and, without thinking, drains the whole thing.

CLARE does.

Sometimes, when the weather was good, or her mother was staying with her aunt, Clare and her father would journey up through the park towards Triglav, the southernmost peak of the Juliske Alps, and camp.

These were the best days. She was in love with the mountains before she could think. And as she grew older she got to know them, face by face, mile by mile. Her father showed her the great glaciers that creaked and sang in the winter, and melted off in the summer. He showed her the flat lakes that sat in the ravines of Skrlatica. He pointed out the hawks that soar over the range's peaks and helped her track the foxes' prints as they dotted their way up the mountain.

Clare sits up, rubs her temple once. Twice.

CLARE sits up and rubs her temples twice. She reaches for the wine.

And refills her glass of wine with a sigh, trying not to think about the last few days.

Sometimes, while they were camping, she and her father would sit by the remains of their cooking fire and her father would tell her stories.

CLARE closes her eyes, almost drifting off to sleep.

He would tell her about the giants that used to live in the caves at Prisojnik. About the remains of the witches coven they found at Pisnica. Once, when he described in such detail the troll that lived by the lake at Razor – about how it would stick goats' bones in a tree and use it as a toothbrush or how it kept a pack of wolves as pets – Clare had spent all night shivering in fear at the side of the tent. When her sobbing had eventually woken her father, the only way he could get her to stop crying was by swearing blindly that he had made the whole thing up. That there was in fact no such thing as the Troll of Razor, that it was just a figment of his imagination, and because of that, there was no need to be scared.

She wakes up.

God, she's knackered. She fell asleep. She dreamed, even, is that possible? Has she woken up, even, she feels dazed.

She pinches herself to check she's awake now.

CLARE pinches herself.

Ow. Her body feels heavy, the weight of it sinking into the chair like she could just sink and sink and disappear. Ugh, she should unpack.

CLARE covers her eyes with her hands.

Guess who?

She'd say.

Guess who it is?

CLARE begins to grin.

Um I don't know who could it be?

Come on guess who?

Is it mum?

Her grin widens.

No!

Is it a bear? A little ugly ogre? Is it a little girl?

Yes!

Is it a funny little girl?

He'd grab her hands and swing her round.

Yes!

CLARE uncovers her eyes still smiling at the memory.

It doesn't look like a girl to me – no no, this looks like a

It is it is!

Like a piglet. Yup, that's what it is, it's a piglet.

He'd swing her over his shoulders; her arms hanging down, barely reaching his belt, is that possible?

Only one thing to do with a piglet.

She'd be giggling

You know what that is don't you?

Laughing against his shoulder as his long strides bounced her up and down

Barbeque it!

The phone vibrates.

The phone buzzes again.

CLARE presses a button.

Beep.

You have three new messages.

Beep

Clare?

Ali ste tam?

Ali ste dobili naše novice tam?

Naši dokumenti ali spletne strani in podobno?

beep

– five to speak to an agent now. Or press nine to opt out and the bank will keep your compensation.

beep

Hi Clare, it's Alexis. Look I'm sorry about how that must have looked. I

I wanted to come to your defence but

I'm not

I'm not quite sure that you understand how it sounds from our point of view that's the thing. These are very experienced people, very rational people, you know.

They're not ready to be

I mean

They don't want to be

I don't know

It was all a bit

Shocking

I s'pose.

It's like. Like. Imagine one of your undergrads suddenly presented a paper saying

Well

Saying that the walls in your flat weren't in fact walls in your flat, that they were

I don't know

Air.

Shit example.

Anyway I hope you're ok.

Beep.

Clare turns the phone over so she can no longer see the screen.

CLARE turns the phone.

She thinks about the message from her mum.

Hi, it said. Are you there? Is anybody home?

73

Clare? Where are you? I'm trying to get through to you.

When are you coming home?

CLARE notices something.

Clare has a rare, effortless elegance.

She reaches for her bare feet and sniffs at them. They stink.

A natural grace that's impossible to teach.

She smells her armpits. They stink too. It's been a long day.

Clare takes off her top and gives herself what her father would call an Albanian shower.

CLARE takes off her top, goes to her bag, rummages through to retrieve the deodorant and sprays it thickly on.

Clare is an extraordinary specimen. Her body, the culmination of years of evolution, stretches and bends. It is capable of great strength and incredible endurance. It is made up of 724 trillion red blood cells and 206 bones.

She's an animal.

She smells.

CLARE puts the deodorant on the table.

There, on her left arm is a scar, about two inches long. A relic from falling out of a tree when she was ten.

And retrieves a rolled up shirt from the backpack.

Somewhere in there is her mind. Not in the backpack, in her skull, encased behind seven millimetres of bone.

CLARE has managed to get tangled up in the shirt.

Capable of incredible processing power. Of poetry, imagination, complex mathematics.

At last, she manages to get it right, redoing the buttons which were the problem.

She's thinking right now.

She buttons up the shirt.

She's having some of her favourite thoughts. The ones where she imagines she's someone else completely.

This is Sophie Dixon. She's a 30 year old personal trainer from London with a lactose intolerance and an addiction to Candy Crush.

This is Cara Supreme. She's a 30 year old NASCAR driver from Missouri. She's totally deaf, which is lucky because her husband's a drummer.

This is Elena Petrova. She's a 30 year old astronaut from Russia with a fear of rats, heights, and commitment.

She should unpack.

One by one CLARE takes a series of objects out of the case and places them offstage in her room. She begins by taking a pile of clothes from the case: clearly mountain-climbing gear: waterproofs and thermals.

For her sixteenth birthday, she and her father planned the longest trip they had been on yet. It was the summer, and a heat wave had melted so much snow that new tracks and routes had opened up all across the mountain.

She takes an academic-looking folder full of papers and writings, and a tangle of phone and laptop chargers.

Halfway through the afternoon of the first day, as they pushed up towards the snowline of the Veliki peaks, Clare realised with horror that she had forgotten their supply of water at the lunch spot, by the lake at Naravni.

She takes three books, revealing them in order: the first two are very heavy academic books, the third is a well-thumbed paperback of 'Fifty Shades Darker'.

Her father was a calm man and they hadn't lost too much time, so he wasn't angry when they decided to turn around. But Clare had been too excited by the day and the weather to remember to drink, and could already feel the dizziness of sunstroke beginning to hit.

She takes equipment from the bag, which is initially fairly innocuous: a thermos, a camping stove, a compass.

The sky melted from blue to red. The sun seemed black. Her father loomed over her as just a panicked blob of colour.

But then increasingly serious: slackline, ratchet straps, crampons, a foot-long ice axe and hammer, which she weighs in her hand.

As he carried her down the hill to the water bottles, her half-open eyes dimly took in a blur of her surroundings. The hazy tree line. The smudge of green grass.

And, something else.

As they reached the lake and her abandoned pack came into view, she would swear blind to her mother when she was finally returned home,

that hunched over her pack,

startled by their return,

was a man.

More than eight feet tall. Feet as large as saucepans. His body, unclothed, but covered from head to foot, in long, matted, white hair.

She takes a handgun from the bag.

Clare goes to the window and reopens the curtains.

CLARE goes to the window, still holding the gun.

She looks down to the street, about thirty feet below her.

The papers say there's a man on the loose.

Escaped and now out there somewhere.

They say he's wild. Dangerous.

He's not here though. Just cars, packed bumper to bumper. A few passers-by – people on their way back from work? On their way to the pub? – but no one else.

There's a knock on Clare's door.

Silence. Then, a knock on the door.

Clare whirls around, surprised. Then, gathering herself, goes to open it.

She goes to the door.

She looks through the peephole.

She opens the door.

77

Whoa don't shoot!

CLARE looks down at the gun and smiles.

Sorry. I forgot I was holding it. Sorry. I'm
unpacking it's not… it's research equipment.
Sorry.

Are you Clare Sahakian?

Yes.

Sign here.

Is that snow?

Yeah. It's really coming down. Here.

He gives her two packages.

*CLARE picks up a package and a smaller letter, pre-set
by the door.*

Thanks.

CLARE returns to the sofa, holding the packages.

She closes the door and goes to the sofa,
holding the packages.

There is no return address. She's not expecting
anything.

She places one on the table and tears the other
open.

She does. It's full of polystyrene flakes.

And inside, are some goggles. The ones she
ordered three months ago.

She takes the goggles from the package and stares at them.

Hours she'd spent online and on the phone
trying to track these things down. Calling
the website, then being put through to the

actual supplier because they don't hold any
stock themselves then being passed on to the
delivery company because blah blah blah. The
delivery company had no record of the order.
No dispatch had been made. There were no
goggles.

And now there were. Where had they been?

She turns them round in her hand.

It was after Clare went to middle school that her
interest in the mountains and the snow became
more than childish. Her understanding began
to deepen into the geological, the physical, the
tectonic. She learned how snow formed and
fell and settled. She learned how rocks became
shaped, how the world became sculpted.

Clare tries the goggles on. Perhaps, she thinks,
if she wears these from now on, no one at the
faculty will recognise me.

Slowly she begins to put the goggles on.

Her Dad had a more imaginative, romantic
view of the mountains and she found herself
increasingly frustrated. She began to make
trips alone, bringing her equipment and her
notebooks. She would stand in the middle
of a blizzard, her fingers freezing, her teeth
chattering, her eyes watching the mountain;
observing, charting, mapping.

Clare wishes she was back there now. The
air. The cold. The whiteness. The walls of her
flat disappear and for a moment she's there,
breathing in the emptiness.

She takes the goggles off.

Suddenly the images of her parents faces are right before her. She sees her mother as she is now, or was when she last saw her. Her eyes lined. Her cheeks wet with tears.

CLARE wipes her eyes.

She sees her father as he was when she was a child. He would have been not much more than her age now, they could be brother and sister. She sees his face older, as he was when she left to come to Cambridge.

It was at Cambridge when she had made her first trip to the arctic. The first time she saw the northern lights she had been standing on the deck of the ship they were taking from Bergen up to Skollsgard. She couldn't believe her eyes, couldn't believe that what she was seeing was real. She understood the science. Understood that the refraction of light in the thinness of the atmosphere led to a dancing, waving, ultraviolet beam.

She understood and yet. Yet. This.

The phone rings.

CLARE's phone begins to vibrate.

Clare picks up the phone and checks the caller. Alexis. How predictable.

CLARE picks up the phone, thinks for a second or two, then presses a button.

She rejects the call.

She goes to the window again and peers out.

She goes to the window.

Still only strangers and the traffic. No wild man on the loose.

She imagines him looking for her.

Following her.

Standing below this window looking up at her.

Watching her. What would he think? Without knowing anything apart from what he could see through that window.

The phone rings again.

The phone vibrates.

This time she answers it.

CLARE stares at the phone for a long time but at length, answers it.

Clare?

Silence.

Clare, talk to me.

Nothing.

Clare, I can understand how you're feel-

I'm fine.

Clare.

Look, I don't want to talk about it ok, if you. If you want to email me or

Clare

There's nothing to say.

Can I come round.

Clare thinks.

I want to talk to you about this properly.

What?

You don't need to be embarrassed.

I'm not embarrassed.

Ok. Well.

You think I should be embarrassed?

That's not what I

Huh?

Said.

Ok. Good.

Beat.

We can't give you the grant Clare.

Fine.

We can't give you money when your proposal,
I mean

I said it's fine

When your paper claims that

Alexis

You have to see it from our perspective

I know what I saw

There's no such thing

And I said I know what I saw

Ok

Well then

There's no such thing

Fine.

Take some time. Go back home for a week.

I know what I saw. I am a scientist.

Clare what you're talking about

I know

What you say you saw

Yes

Is the abominable snowman.

Silence.

Let me come over Clare. Please. I want to see you face to face.

Why?

Wh- I want to check you're ok.

There's a pause. Clare thinks.

Silence.

CLARE nods.

Whatever.

Clare hangs up the phone and waits for Alexis to arrive.

CLARE puts the phone down and paces the room in a circle.

She puts on the radio.

The radio begins to play as CLARE paces. Classical muzak, on a low volume.

She walked into the room. A room of men sitting the other side of three tables pushed together, staring at her. Always men, she

thought, even now it's always fucking men.
Deciding what I do, handing out my pocket
money.

She had a grant to undertake three research
trips to the Alps to monitor the glaciers. It was
the second that had caused the problems she
was now facing.

She heads to the kitchen to get something to
eat. The voice on the radio reminds her of her
father, so she hits it off as she goes past.

CLARE exits. The radio stops.

The frame of the man, silhouetted against the
sun, squinting up at him, grinning.

He had wanted her to go to university. He had
been proud when she'd got into Cambridge –
he'd heard of Cambridge. She wanted him to
see her as a success. She was pleased that he
did.

The cupboards are bare.

*CLARE returns with a biscuit and an apple. Beat. She
sits in the chair and begins to eat the biscuit.*

Sometimes she'd sneak up behind him and try
to lift *him* up. She'd heave against his calves like
trying to uproot tree trunks. Peering up at his
frame, wrapping her arms around saying my
turn this time my turn I'm going to carry you,
carry you to the barbecue!

Great, I'd love a lift, he'd say as she heaved
against his legs.

When are you going to start trying?

She'd collapse to the floor, panting with the effort. Well? Where's that lift then?

CLARE begins to eat one of the biscuits.

Yes it was the second trip that had caused the problem.

Arriving at base camp, looking around her at those familiar peaks and valleys. Being proud to show them off to her research assistants. Waving away their earnest attempts to get out the GPS. She tramped ahead, confidently leading them up

Up

Up

Toward Velico Spicje, smirking into her face protector as their numb fingers struggled with zips. This was home.

She begins to massage her feet, like she's massaging the day away.

It was on the first morning that she saw them.

She had got up early, wanting to have some time on her own before the others were awake. She wanted some time to look out at the view. To remember. To think.

Lots of her colleagues pushed for the modern trend towards collective research, but Clare preferred to sit in silence and think. She didn't have to be alone, as in, physically alone. She could think just as well in silent company. Like on her walks with her father. They had rarely needed to talk the day away, but had both been content in their own thoughts. Their own thoughts but – crucially – inspired by the same landscape. For that was a different kind of silence. Their thoughts, though undiscussed, were somehow harmonious – were vibrating on the same frequency. They would often stop for a snack and some water halfway through the morning and her father would verbalise some seemingly random thought,

Do you think a cow has a best friend?

Only for Clare to confirm that she had been wondering the exact same thing.

She knew that as soon as her assistants were up the time for contemplation would be over. Half an hour of peace to think about how best to organise the day. Snow was already beginning to fall, which would make it hard to get up much higher than they already were.

She noticed the fire in the centre of camp.

They had left it burning to ward off foxes during the night.

The snow was beginning to fall harder as she approached, blinking back her confusion.

The remains of the fire had been scattered, as if by an animal. The burnt out logs and remains of charcoal clearly and haphazardly spread all over the camp.

But that wasn't what was confusing her. She stared beyond the fire, where she could see, already being covered by a thick blanket of snow, tracks leading into the camp and then back away, into the distance.

Clare stumbled forward. Shaking the snow out of her eyes, telling herself it was a fox or even a hare, but as soon as she reached the fire, she knew it was him again.

The vision of that fever dream all those years ago came back.

Not a dream.

Real.

The tracks at her feet, filling with dusty snowflakes, were no fox, and they were no hare. They were human, only far larger. The big toe clearly delineated, the ball of the foot visible as a deeper impression into the soft powder.

She placed her boot – already comfortably larger than her actual foot – into the print. There were at least three inches space on every side. The toes were flat and round, with no clear indentation of a claw.

And most importantly: there were no hind prints. These tracks were bipedal. Upright.

The animal had walked in.

And walked out.

Suddenly, her faculties came back to her. She stumbled through the thick snow back to her tent. What had she been thinking – becoming a child again and not a scientist. She tore open the tent and scrambled inside, trying to find the camera she knew was buried deep inside her bag.

At last she found it and, scrabbling back to her feet and out into the snow again, falling even harder now, she called to her assistants.

Max!

Toby!

By the time she made it back to the fire, crucial minutes had passed and already the tracks had filled with fresh snow, leaving the indentation hazy and vague. Some of the footprints had all but disappeared entirely.

Toby!

Max!

Already a part of her – a voice in her head – knew that it was crucial that someone else apart from her saw these.

Come on!

She fumbled with her camera, trying to get her thick ski gloves to work the fiddly little buttons. Her swearing bursting staccato clouds of steam into the snow.

She ripped off the gloves and turned the camera on. She snapped manically at the footprints, trying desperately to find the best one left but already she could tell that the snow and the dawn light was flattening the prints, that the extraordinary was being dulled. Even without consulting the screen she could already feel the scepticism of the photos. The blurriness. The whiteness. It was the same scepticism she would have felt of someone else.

An honest mistake.

A bear maybe? Unable to hibernate and lost on the mountain.

What is it?

Max had managed to stumble, sleepy, from his tent.

Are you ok?

I…?

He wandered over, zipping his outer and pulling up his hood.

Jesus it's foul out here. Are you alright?

Clare looked at the tracks but there was nothing left.

Professor? What's the emergency.

The snow had flattened out the land, smoothed it over for the new day.

She stared at the virgin snow, she tried to conjure the prints back with her mind, or to wonder whether Max could possibly still see them if she tried to explain.

Clare?

But they were gone.

Nothing. She said. I just want to get started.

A car horn beeps loudly outside the window.

Clare goes to the window and looks down to the street below.

Outside the window, stretching out Eastward over towards the horizon, is the East of Cambridge. Shopping streets and old colleges all the way up to Mill Road. Then houses, thousands upon thousands of them dissolving into fields. Cherry Hinton. Bury St Edmunds. Ipswich. Low-lying fenland and reclaimed bogs, flat and dark and now dusted with snow.

And then beyond that, the Suffolk coast. The sea. Black and deep and cold. Then Holland. Europe. Asia. The World.

All spanning out from here. From this room.

CLARE looks out of the window. A long time passes.

She looks out of the window.

And somewhere out there

This man on the loose.

CLARE goes to the back and digs a penknife from it, flicking out the blade. She returns to the seat, picks up the apple and begins to slice bits off and eat them.

Traces.

Traces of snow in rock.

Traces of ice as it scratched and dragged it's mass across the mountains.

Clare had spent her adult life running her fingers across the surfaces of stone trying to feel for the jags, the edges, the fault lines. Where one geological era met another, where one glacier butted up against another.

How the ice left traces on the world was her speciality. It was her thing. People too. Her first dissertation as an undergraduate had been slammed by her supervisor for failing to take into account the effect of the last thousand years

90

on her area of study. For failing to take into account ourselves, herself. Her own footprints. Her own breath.

Had she not realised, Professor Ellis had said, looking at her as if only a woman, only a girl could make such a basic, near-sighted mistake, that her own body would effect the area around the test site. She had *fiddled* – he almost spat the word – she had been back too often to check, too mistrustful of the equipment to leave it alone in the landscape. Had she not realised, he said again, that her body would effect the earth? That human bodies scar and scratch and heat just like glaciers.

No.

No she hadn't realised that.

Why not?

CLARE takes up the knife and runs it across her palm.

Because she felt like she didn't. Was that it?

Tracing a pathway along her skin.

She had felt somehow light. Unreal. Unable to impact the earth. Unable to make those traces. Is that not how we are, she thought? Is that not really how we are? We don't scratch and drag ourselves like glaciers. We slip off the surface of the world without disruption, softly, silent as shaken snow.

CLARE stands up.

Clare sat down.

CLARE takes a drink of wine.

91

Clare sat down and closed her eyes.

CLARE stands and breathes deeply. Then, sits and does what the NARRATOR says.

She puts her feet up and composes herself. She thinks about how to calm things down. How to put things right.

She's left the window open and the refreshing, cold air gives her goosebumps. She reaches for her jacket.

CLARE pulls her jacket from her bag and pulls it around her.

She thinks about the third day of the trip.

A storm had set in. The camp had been whited out and she had sent her two assistants to bolt down the equipment at the site. She would stay here and secure the camp.

The sleet was near horizontal.

Even with her jacket zipped tight, and her hat pulled close over her goggles, the snow still lashed at her cheeks. She began to batten down the guy ropes and weigh down the inside of the tents to make sure they didn't blow away. The snow pelted her goggles and visibility was near-zero.

She expected the others back soon and began to glance to where they'd be coming from, hoping to see them when they got close.

Pulling the generator towards the cluster of tents she saw something, approaching from their direction.

She shouted out to them, but knew that the wind would blow the sound back at her. She squinted out through her goggles, looking for the shape.

The snow swirled. The wind howled.

Then, the shape appeared again.

It wasn't her assistants.

It was a man.

What was a man doing climbing alone in this?

Just a shadow at first, but it was moving towards her, towards the camp.

She stumbled towards it. He would need help.

A squall in the storm. A brief respite, and Clare wiped her goggles clean.

She saw the shape more clearly.

He was about twenty yards away. She could see him.

More than eight feet tall.

White, matted hair covering his naked body from head to foot.

He stood upright on two thin legs. He saw her. He looked at her.

They looked at each other.

His eyes were black. His muzzle half-human-half bear.

The sasquatch.

The yeti.

The abominable.

She blinked. And there he still was.

This wasn't a hallucination. It wasn't a glimpse in a storm or a shadow in the middle of the night. She was looking at it. It was looking at her.

Seconds passed.

She looked it over. She looked at how the fur gathered at it's ankles. She looked at the muzzle, bear-like but with the flatness, the personality of a human. She looked at the hands, large as tennis rackets, clawed and ragged. She looked at it's eyes. Into it's eyes. Black pebbles, like teddy-bears' eyes.

This wasn't an apparition. She was looking straight at it.

This is what she had tried to explain to everyone. To her students when they came back. To Alexis on the phone when they got back to camp. To her friends when she returned home. And now here, to her supervisors at the other end of a desk.

It's just

She hadn't glimpsed it.

This kind of thing

She hadn't spotted it from afar

Isn't real

She had watched it.

Does that make sense? How can we credit it when only you saw it?

But what does that matter to her? To Clare? *She* had seen it. *She* knows she saw it. She knows that she's not mad. What can you trust if you can't trust yourself? If you can't see something,

Feel something,

Look at something and know what it is? Her whole life had been built on that assumption. That she could look at something and make a judgement.

The tracks?

A bear, if that. Half covered in snow by the time the team came back.

The photos?

Smudged, blurry, distant. Too easy to photoshop or explain away.

The teeth marks in her chocolate bar. Handed to it, held out and offered to it as if she were feeding a pet?

A human bite. Hers probably. And if not, one of the students. Too crumbled, melted and cracked to get a proper mould from by the time it got home.

But *she* knew. She knew because she saw it. She saw it like she saw the table in front of her right now. But what does that even mean?

Clare rubs her eyes.

CLARE rubs her eyes.

Yes.

What does that even mean?

She snaps to the window. And the sound of outside fades, like the window's been closed.

Clare had received the call on a Thursday night and could hear immediately in her mother's voice that something was wrong.

She removes her jacket and puts it back on the bag.

24 hours later she was in Kolmin, sitting with her mother face to face.

CLARE sits on the sofa staring out.

They sat opposite each other in her parent's living room. Her old living room.

A small table. Some scattered magazines. A chair. The photo of her father in military uniform sitting on the mantelpiece.

Clare stared at the photo, trying to detect a change in him, a change in the way she felt about him. Had there been a sign, even then, of betrayal? Is that a twinkle she now sees in his eyes? Is that slight smile, that turn at the corners of his mouth, the comforting, trustworthy smile she had always thought. Or is it the smile of a secret? The smile of something hidden.

Her mother busied herself around the house. Making tea, fixing lunch, putting fresh sheets on Clare's bed.

How was the trip?

Good, fine.

How is work?

Mum.

She stared at her mother's face. What was she thinking? Could you tell anything about someone just from looking at them? Why wasn't she crying? Why wasn't she showing anything? She just sat there, blankly.

The longer they sat there the less she felt she knew what was going on inside that head.

Eventually, her mother said.

We have to be strong.

We?

We're a family.

No. Not any more.

He's still the same person. He's still your father.

Mum.

How can you think you know someone so well and have it taken away from you so quickly? Was she that gullible? All her life she had known this man. She had seen him act. She had looked at his face. She had believed it when his friends told her what a great dad she had. She had

She had

Believed.

And then this.

Her mother in one ear. A pub quiz babbling in the other.

Clare.

Is that you?

It's your father.

I think. I think you should come home.

Why?

I just.

What's happened?

She remembered rowing across the Bohinjsko.
She remembered camping at Zlatorog.

He's been arrested.

She remembered toasted marshmallows and
boiled dumplings on the camp fire.

It doesn't look good.

And now she was hearing this. Those trips.
Those mountains. Those woods. Not nature
trails after all. Not a chance to press flowers or
follow tracks. A chance to scout routes, to map
directions. So that when he went out alone
he would be prepared. So he could meet his
contacts at Polje. Take the girls off their hands,
five, six at a time, and lead them through the
woods, through the night, to the Italian border.

She had trusted him.

She had known him.

Stop looking at me like that.

Stop looking at me like that, she thought.

Who am I? Does everyone get this? Who the
fuck

Like

How did I end up here?

My father took me out to the woods. He told me the difference between stairstep and feather moss, how you boil one and eat the other raw. He taught me to use binoculars and look at the clouds to tell what the weather was going to be. He told me to look and to learn and to imagine and then twenty five years later I'm here. Is it that simple? I do what I'm told just because I'm told.

Clare reaches for her phone.

CLARE presses some buttons on her phone.

Music begins to play.

Sound begins to play.

It is odd. A deep, meditative hum, unusual and unworldly and yet, in a strange way, comforting.

At first it had been a joke.

Paula had given it to her at the faculty secret santa. She could tell it was Paula by the wink as she unwrapped it. Everyone laughed as she held it up.

She wasn't even going to bother actually listening but then that night, struggling to get to sleep as her father appeared again and again in the room, she got up and put it on.

It was the sound of glaciers moving.

She lay in bed surrounded by the sound of that continental shift. The singing, humming force of the ice cracking around her.

Since then, she has grown to like it, even need it. And she puts it on now to calm her, to take her away from the room. This room.

He only came here once, nearly two years ago. He held the door open as her mother fussed in and pottered about. Instantly moving things round and minutely adjusting the things that Clare had carefully

Anxiously?

Placed before they arrived.

Clare watched as her father came in.

Had he shrunk slightly? He looked smaller than she remembered.

Clare almost held her breath as he took in the place. She wanted him to notice the photo of the Triglav peak she had framed on the coffee table, and the doctorate on the wall. She had brought her old childhood blanket out from her bedroom and folded neatly as a throw on the sofa. She hoped he would like that she still thought of home, even in this room, so far away.

He looked around the room. This room. And said

Kje jegasilni aparat?

Where's the fire extinguisher?

Clare realised that she had never even looked for a fire extinguisher. Just as her father hadn't noticed the sentimental objects from home, or the frustrating way the repainted window frame didn't match the door. It was as if they were seeing a different room altogether.

Her mother returned from the kitchen and said

Bog je prašen tukaj

God it's dusty in here.

Clare reaches again for the wine and takes a long sip.

CLARE drinks.

She wanted him to see her as a success. She was pleased that he did.

She wanted people to look at her and see something to see

What

A success

A scientist

A woman

A daughter

A

But what was hers? What was that part of her that people couldn't see?

Was there a part of her that was truly private, that was truly personal, a part that could not be communicated or judged from the outside?

CLARE sits, perhaps on the verge of tears.

Clare had looked at her mother. Looked at her as she began to weep. She'd said to her, why are you crying? Why are you crying when you're not sad? You can't feel that for him, not now. You don't need to show everyone how upset you are. So stop acting like a little kid!

Her mother's bedroom door was ajar. She could hear a noise from inside. Praying. She and her dad used to catch each other's eye when her mum prayed before meals. Please watch over us.

Why?

Why did she get so much comfort from being watched? And what could watching tell you anyway? Clare was watching her mother right now and seeing what? Hunched shoulders. Clasped hands. Empty.

People like her mother feel the need to show emotion at times like this. Why? Sometimes the biggest moments of our lives happen in private,

in silence,

with nothing more visible than the tap of a keyboard or the closing of a book. Isn't that ok?

The glacier track ends.

'Ice Ice Baby' starts playing.

Paula had added that to the playlist as a joke.

There's a loud knock at the door. CLARE wheels round. She turns the music off.

Clare? It's me, Alexis.

CLARE stares at the door. Silence.

In 1846 a man brought back a Kiwi from New Zealand to England and everyone thought it was a hoax.

She continues to look at the door.

They thought he had made the whole thing up.

CLARE stares at the door.

Eventually the Royal Society disbarred him and he left in disgrace.

Clare? Are you there?

A long pause.

Clare I know you're in there, I could see the light from the street.

Clare I want to help you.

I'm your friend.

How can I help you if you won't let me see you.

I don't need help.

Silence.

Look

I have photos

CLARE picks up the stack of papers from the table and takes them towards the door.

I know

I have records, other pe

You've shown them to me.

So

I've seen them Clare.

Silence. CLARE clutches her records, and slumps down next to the door.

Please let me in.

Pause.

Clare, Alexis says, I think you need to see someone.

Why?

Because you're imagining things.

Clare stares at the papers in her hands.
Records, photos, journals. Accounts by others
who've seen similar. Photographs decades old
of footprints like hers. All myths, she thinks, all
myths have their origin in something once seen.

Clare?

You don't believe these photographs?

They're barely shapes Clare. At best they could
be an animal but frankly

Do you believe I saw something?

Yes, of course but

Do you believe I saw a shape that looked like a
man?

Why are you doing this?

Do you believe I believe I saw this animal?

Clare

Because I need to know where you stop. Why
do you believe me when I say some things
and not others. Why are some things more
believable to you than others?

Because other people can corroborate them.
Other people I trust.

Clare can feel her on the other side of the door.

Why don't you believe me?

Clare.

I'm not a liar.

Let me in.

I'm not a liar.

Out in the corridor, Alexis says: look, I'm on your side, ok. I understand the need to create these kinds of creatures. We all do it. We're all afraid of – 'out there'. It's a natural impulse. When we're not sure of something, when we're afraid. That's why people create these wild men. Out of fear.

Clare sees her mother. Her shoulders hunched, her hands clasped.

No.

Fear that beyond what you can see is something you can't control.

Clare says: No. I'm not afraid.

Silence.

You're not going to let me in?

Silence.

Ok. Well…

Silence.

Listen, and I'm saying this as a friend, ok, as someone who cares a lot about you. Maybe you are telling the truth but, I'm sorry, I'm really sorry but… that's not enough.

You have a choice Clare: either you stay here and accept the decision, or,

Or you bring us something we can see for ourselves.

Pause.

Alexis leaves, and Clare is alone.

CLARE looks at the papers.

She looks through some of them.

She holds one of them, and rips it in half. Resigned, she lets the rest drop to the floor. It's over.

Out there.

Out there all alone.

Maybe the last of it's kind.

The last.

Wandering in the wilderness and nothing to

No one to

Her father had taught her about the animals that used to walk the mountains millions and millions of years ago. Rodents five feet tall that dammed rivers and carved out trenches. Sabre toothed cats, with canines as big and sharp as carving knives. And her favourite, the woolly mammoth. The gentle, hulking, furry elephant, plodding great distances across the snow and ice.

The poor, wretched animal.

The last of the papers in her hands she takes to the table and drops there. As she does, she notices the other letter, delivered earlier.

She takes it up.

She knows the handwriting. Recognises the mountains and stars of the Slovenian stamps.

CLARE stares at the envelope.

She half thinks about throwing it away
unopened. Denying him the chance to speak,
would that make a difference?

She opens it.

And reads it.

If you would just listen

A chance to explain

I just want to

I need to try to

Just because people have said

Just because

Don't believe everything

Anything.

You hear.

I love you

I'm still here

The words seem to melt from the page and
leave nothing.

Silence.

CLARE puts down the letter and picks up her phone.
She looks at it, takes a deep breath and begins to dial.

She will call Alexis and apologise. She will
arrange to come in tomorrow and admit that
she has been under stress. She will tell them
about her father and everything and convince
them to give her another chance. She will stop
all this talk.

She hovers over the last button.

The thought made her feel sick. Having to stand on ceremony.

Ugh. Could she send someone else? Could she just hire someone to go in her place? To stand there and get stared at.

She presses it.

And she could be elsewhere.

The phone begins to ring.

Away from all of them.

Ring.

They would never know that they were with just

Ring.

Just

Ring.

A body.

Ring.

She looks at the letter, still clutched in her hand.

Hello?

The handwriting, a scrawl, barely readable.

Hello?

A sentence towards the end. A dream. A memory.

Is anyone there?

A description of that hot day all those years ago.

The lake at Naravni. Him carrying her back to camp.

Hello?

His favourite he says his favourite place of all.

CLARE hangs up the phone.

She stares at the letter.

She looks at the phone.

Maybe she doesn't apologise. Yes. Maybe she goes to find the creature. Yes.

CLARE types another number on the phone and lets it ring.

They don't believe you? Well go and find it yourself.

The ringing stops.

Hi. I'd like a car please as soon as you can send one.

She'll find the animal, take better photos, find better prints.

65 Circus Road you can just call me from outside.

She'll bring him back for everyone to see.

That's fine. I'll be here.

To the airport. I need a cab to the airport.

She hangs up.

She has to pack.

CLARE begins to pack, quickly, urgently.

The trial had been a big story in the local newspaper, and was reported in the national press too. The journalists had not been kind to her father.

She begins to put things in the bag...

'Drawn and haggard'

'Visibly tired'

'Without visible sign of remorse or sorrow'.

Visible sign.

Visible.

...Some assorted clothes...

What did they want? Her father had not shed a tear at his mother's funeral. He did not 'visibly express' emotion. Did that mean he did not feel it? Did that mean he wasn't feeling regret or sorrow or any of those things?

No.

Or.

Maybe.

How did she know?

...The ice equipment...

His face his body language had, all the way through the trial, been calm. Relaxed even. Every one in the courtroom, maybe two hundred people, staring at him all day every day for three weeks, imposing thoughts onto his blank face.

Angry.

Sad.

Regretful.

Proud.

Maybe. Maybe all of them.

She had done the same with the jury. Looking at their faces, trying to read their reactions.

Disbelieving?

Vengeful?

Bored?

…The gun…

But after a week she had given up. It was too difficult. She could not know.

CLARE zips up the backpack. She holds it.

Guilty.

At the end of the trial he looked over to Clare and her mother but still there was no visible emotion. Something had changed though. That word, more than an opinion now, a fact. Impossible to deny or to clean off. This was what he was.

Like father,

or husband

or man. This was a fact now.

She takes her camera from the top of the bag.

You can only lie with words. That's a fact. You can't lie with your body. An animal can't lie. A mountain can't lie.

She takes some test pictures of the audience to check that it's working.

You can tell yourself lies. I'm not angry. I'm not upset. I'm not myself today.

But no amount of words can make you actually *be* someone else.

She puts the camera back in the bag.

Or be somewhere else.

She zips up the bag and closes the padlock, twisting the numbered dials around.

The last time she saw him was in prison. She had visited the night he was convicted, before he was transferred to the prison in Kranj.

She takes a deep breath.

She had been allowed to stand outside his cell, with him inside, talking through a window in the door, a guard standing about five yards behind her.

She turns to the set and begins to dismantle it.

When the window opened he had looked up at her,
and she had smiled, instinctively.

She takes the table apart and scatters the papers and polystyrene from the package over the floor.

He came close to her, on the other side of the window, having to stoop a little to keep his face in view.

She had waited for him to speak.

It seemed like minutes.

At last he said

You have to believe me.

Why?

Because – I'm telling you.

She picks up her coat puts it on, zipping and fastening it tight, standing in the middle of the scattered paper and polystyrene flakes, covering the stage in white. It could almost be snow.

And now she's ready.

The glacier music restarts.

She takes up her bag and gets a cab to the airport.

She gets a plane to Dubrovnik and a bus to the hills.

She takes her backpack from the bus and pulls her coat above her ears.

She doesn't even wait in Bohinskja long enough to see whether there's a room for the night but sets off directly past the bus station, past the gym, past the outdoor wear shops and past the final bar before the road thins out to just an unlit track leading up into the hills.

She begins to walk in ever contracting circles around the stage.

This is no night to be out, especially alone. The wind is up, the snow is swirling. Even in the village snow had been banked up on the pavement nearly a foot thick. Cars slipping on the road, even with chains.

Clare pulls her jacket closer and presses on.

How can you not see that?

How can you

How can you

How can you be so

So

So

Dense.

Snow whirls around her head.

Horizontal sleet makes her eyes blink and her hair freeze into clumps.

She wheels around.

Nothing but the wind

Nothing but the ice and the whiteness and the

How can you bury your heads in your research like this I feel like

Like

Like I'm fucking talking to

I'm *telling* you it happened, isn't that good for something?

Can't you *see* it when I talk about it?

Don't you see it here with you?

She doesn't need them. She doesn't need their money. She's been on these hills all her life before she had even heard of Scott or grants or Cambridge.

This is her home. These are her mountains. And she can find him herself.

She blinks the snow away. Yes. She puts the goggles on and presses onwards, upwards.

By the time she reaches the plateau at Malo Spikje it is deep into the night. She has broken through the cloud line and now there is nothing between her and the sky.

She has reached the centre of the stage. She turns slowly around, searching.

The cold is freezing the moisture of her breath even as it rises, so that it sparkles like diamond dust in front of her eyes.

She breathes again, just to see that magic.

No, not magic.

Not.

She pulls her coat around her. The plateau is no bigger than a room, cascading into the abyss on all sides in jutting intervals. No bigger than a room. A room in a small apartment.

The wind whistles across the surface, whipping up little clouds of snow, disrupting the most recent fall.

Her eyes begin to grow heavy. She blinks slowly. Is her body shutting down. It was a mistake to come on her own.

She fights the temptation to fall to her knees.

She fights the temptation to pretend any more.

She fights the voice in her head that is telling her she came to find proof when she knows

She knows

In the gloom of the night she can see the silver outline of the Veliki peaks

And she knows where she has to go.

She presses onwards. Stumbling. Running.

Words press in on her mind, on her body. Words in the trial, in the newspapers:

Husband,

Father,

Guilty.

And then new words. Not just guilty now.

Loose.

Dangerous.

Photos of crumpled metal and deep scratch marks in the ice-covered roads; the tyre chains ripped and twisted; the windscreen glass scattered even to the other side of the road.

Running.

Black ice lit by the flashes of the ambulance. Two of the transported prisoners and the driver dead on arrival. The second officer still breathing; his eyes open, watching, unsure of his own vision. A shape.

Running.

The doors of the van smashed open. And on the road, footprints. Traces.

I couldn't be sure. It looked like it. He was upright. Hurt but upright. He crossed the road.

The footprints led in that direction too.

Disappeared into the trees I'm sorry I was hurt I couldn't

Bloody footprints tracing out of the ruined van. Across the icy road. Into the silence of the snow. The night. The trees. Then up

Up

Up

Towards the mountains of his home.

And fading. Disappearing with the soft and shuffling snowfall.

Only a man who knew those mountains

Only a man who could survive up there

Who knew how to cover his tracks and hunt for food

Who knew the difference between stairstep and feather moss, how you must boil the first and eat the second raw.

I saw him, he said. I wanted to follow him but. But I was hurt. He was hurt. He couldn't he couldn't he couldn't get far.

Running, stumbling.

CLARE reaches down and picks up the letter from the floor, looking at it, clutching it in her hand.

His strong arms. The heat of a fever dream. Their place. Their favourite place.

She drops the letter.

A body.

A body out there alone. Hurt. Shivering.

Alone in the wilderness.

The NARRATOR stands up from his chair.

There's a man out there.

Somewhere out there.

On the loose.

And she's going to find him.

She forces herself onwards.

Onwards through the night and the snow and the cold until she can see the deeper blackness of what can only be the lake, frozen over into a great black pupil in the eye of the snow.

Is it a bear?

No!

Is it a little ugly ogre?

No!

Is it a little girl?

Yes!

Is it a funny little girl?

She stumbles to their camping spot, a jutting outcrop of flat land to the east of the water. She tries to run, tripping and staggering to the place. She is nearly there, close enough to see by the light of the moon.

A girl.

Close enough that the light from the stars, reflecting off the packed snow, illuminates the area so that she can see

Nothing.

Emptiness.

Just her, alone.

A funny little girl.

She howls at the moon like a lost animal. Alone in the wilderness. The last of her kind.

Her breath runs out and she sobs to herself.

The NARRATOR gets up from his chair and enters the stage, behind CLARE.

And then, through the silence, she hears him.

CLARE turns, until she is face to face with the NARRATOR.

A mound of snow, a little further off. A makeshift camp. A snowhole. And as she approaches, the sound of a shivering, whimpering breath.

Clare approaches the hole. She looks inside and he's there. Right in front of her eyes.

He's hurt and weak, but he's alive. He's here.

He knew she'd come. He knew she'd help him run. Only she would know how he could never live in a cage. How it was better to live alone in the wilderness as a monster than be stared at and spoken about and misjudged.

CLARE: But that isn't why she's here.

They look at each other.

He looks up.

He looks up and out of the hole.

He feels the cramping of his frostbitten legs and the scratching of his frozen breath. He feels his body broken and his mind begin to swim with the cold.

He looks up and in the space above he sees a figure, looming upwards towards the black of the sky. Over eight feet tall. The moon behind making her hair glow white against the night sky.

She looks at him: helpless, feeble, scared.
He looks at her: a lonely creature lost in the wilderness. They look at each other.

He says to her: You're here.

She says to him: Yes. I'm here.

They look at each other. The noise of the glaciers and the wind begins to rise.

Why? He says.

Because it's time now. Time for me to carry you.

I'm going to carry you home.

She feels tall. She feels strong.

She heaves his broken body from the hole and manages to hoist him to her shoulders. She is carrying him. She stumbles forward and then rights herself. She is balanced.

She carries him away from the camp and down the hill.

She carries him past the snowline and onto the road.

She nearly buckles with the weight but pushes on. She carries him downwards, through the night. At times she has to stop for rest. At times she can barely move him and at others her legs buckle with his weight.

But together they make their way down

Down

Down

Towards Triglav. Towards justice. Towards knowledge and the future.

While behind them,

Far behind them,

Up in the snow high high above

Amongst the giants of Prisojnik and the trolls of Razor

She knows that something is still there.

Someone is still there.

She knows because she saw him. And even if she can never prove it she'll still know because what they had up there

What she saw

What she felt

Was real.

The two of them stare at each other.

The sound of the glacier rises and rises and rises.

HEATHER

Heather (originally '*Helen*') was first performed at the Tobacco Factory on 15th April August 2014 and featured the following cast and creative team:

A	Timothy X Atack
B	Charlotte Melia
Directed by	Valentina Ceschi
Sound by	Timothy X Atack

The production was then revived for a national tour and a run at the Bush Theatre and featured the following cast and creative team:

A	Ashley Gerlach
B	Charlotte Melia
Directed by	Valentina Ceschi
Produced by	Paul Jellis
Designed by	Lily Arnold
Lighting by	Joe Price
Sound by	Iain Armstrong

Heather is a play written for two actors, A and B. The two actors don't play the parts as such, but rather deliver the parts to the audience. The fact of what the actors look like is sort of immaterial; indeed, in some ways the contrast between the voice in the play and the speaker in the room is the fun of it.

A and B don't necessarily have to be the same actor all the way through. You may decide it is most interesting if one actor always plays A. But you might think it's more interesting if she plays A then B then A again. Up to you.

1. SELECTED EMAILS

A   Dear Ms. Eames,

Thank you for sending me the manuscript for *Greta and the Pen of the Necromancer.* I'm glad that Jonathan recommended me – he's a dear friend – so thank you (and him!) for those kind words.

To cut to the chase, I found Greta to be a revelation. If this is, as you say, your first novel, then I think you have a long career ahead of you! It's not perfect – there are some issues and characters I would like to discuss with you (I'm not certain about Drexler, the Lord of the Wolves, who feels a trifle derivative) – but overall I found it to be witty, sharply plotted and the characters charmingly drawn. I agree with what you said in your covering letter that it's not a 'children's book' but, in my opinion those distinctions matter less and less.

Would you be available to come to my offices in London to discuss the book? We would very much like to talk to you about developing and, hopefully, publishing it some time in the future?

All the best,

Harry Purville

B   Dear Harry,

Thank you so much for your kind words – I'm over the moon!

I probably shouldn't mention this but I have had a number of less enthusiastic responses from publishers so I can't tell you what it means to me to hear praise for Greta! I can honestly say she feels like a daughter to me so it hurts when people are mean to her ;)

Thank you also for mentioning your fears about Drexler. My original intention was to provide a threat to the Butterfly Fields and created Drexler to do this, but I agree that as it turned out, he felt a little tired. Instinctively I wonder if it might help if I took out his enchanted collar?

My only piece of bad news is that I won't be able to come to London to meet you. I am very pregnant (my other daughter ;)) and don't feel comfortable being too far away from my doctor. Oh, and my husband!

If we could continue to talk via email for the time being that would be great for me.

All the best,

Heather

A   Dear Heather,

Thank you for replying so swiftly. Of course I understand about the pregnancy – I'm sure we can move forward without a visit if we're both happy.

In short, we would like to purchase the rights to publish the book. I would then handle the editing personally and we would work towards a final draft for publication. For all this we would be able to offer you a £5000 advance set against the royalties.

If all this sounds palatable to you I will have our business affairs people get in touch with you and we can send a contract over ASAP.

All the best,

Harry

B   Hi Harry,

This all sounds wonderful – how exciting!

With any luck there'll be two great pieces of news within a few weeks of each other.

All the best,

Heather xx

A   Hi Heather,

Thanks for returning my call earlier, sorry you had to go but I appreciate time is short in the circumstances!

I hope all the notes made sense – please give me another call if you need to clarify anything.

Looking forward to the revised draft.

All the best and love to Caroline too,

Harry

B   Dear Harry,

Please find attached the new draft. Sorry for the delay, it proved a little more difficult than I thought – if only *I* had a magic pen!

All the best,

Heather

A   Dearest Heather,

I couldn't be happier, I think these changes have made the difference. I'm very happy to 'let the Dragon out of the witch's coven'!

H xx

B   Harry,

What happy news, I'm thrilled.

It couldn't come at a better time for me. I have been rather ill I'm afraid. Without going into details my doctor tells me it is quite serious. It certainly feels that way I'm afraid and I have been stuck in bed for the last few weeks. It's only Caroline and thoughts of the next Greta book that cheer me up.

Please keep me up to date with all the progress toward publication. I'm so excited and only sorry I can't be a part of it in person.

All the best,

H xx

A   Gosh Heather,

I'm so sorry to hear you're ill. Please don't let this be an extra stress on you. I have a lot of experience with this sort of thing so I'm sure we can handle things our end and of course we will keep you up to date with everything.

H xx

| A | Dear Heather,

Attached is the draft of the cover – what do you think!

Personally, I'm in love with it. I think Serge has really captured Greta's spirit and the gold leaf is even more resplendent than I imagined it! What you don't get with the PDF of course is the fact that the motes of magic dust coming from Greta's pen will be slightly embossed.

I hope you're as pleased as we all are!

Lots of love,

H xx

| B | Dear Harry,

It's everything I wanted.

Thank you,

H

| A | Wonderful! Full steam ahead!

H xx

| B | Dear Harry,

I've just received the books through the post! What a wonderful surprise! I have been feeling a bit down recently, not at all myself, and this was exactly what I needed! I have been staring at them ever since!

Well, that's eight gone, just need another 2992 to sell and we'll have to do a second edition ;)

Love,

H xx

A   Dear Heather,

I hope you're feeling better, it was good to chat, albeit briefly, just now, thank you for calling.

Our initial offer to the major booksellers – Waterstones, Tescos and Foyles so far – has been met with a great deal of enthusiasm, and Tescos in particular are interested in a point of sale promotion, which would be amazing for a first timer. As I mentioned just now, Amazon are already getting a lot of positive feedback on the message boards.

I don't want to get our hopes up but I have to confess, the omens are good.

Fingers crossed,

Harry xxx

A   Oh Heather,

What a star you are! I hope you are making progress with the second Greta book because the first is, if you'll forgive the pun, flying!

The notices – we've had the *Times*, *Sunday Telegraph* and the *London Evening Standard Magazine* half term reads special so far – have been glowing and, more importantly, the word online is fantastic. Waterstones have already ordered more and Amazon are restocking too.

My darling – it's a hit!

I do hope you are well enough to come
down to London for a celebration meal –
Ian of course too if you can bear to leave
Caroline with someone – or if not I must
come up to you to raise a glass!

Harry

B   Dear Harry,

What fantastic news. I know I mustn't but
I'm already fantasising about private schools
and round the world trips for Caroline!

I'm afraid I really can't come to London
and I must insist that you don't come up
here. I hate to be so vain, but I just hate the
thought of my illness getting involved in all
this. I can't tell you how nice it is to have
something completely separate!

I hope you understand. Long may this
continue,

Lots of love,

H xx

A   Dear Heather,

I hope you're feeling a bit better. I'm sorry
to inundate you with calls when you're so
fragile. It's hard to express quite how much
demand there is for interviews or public
appearances. Not to sound vulgar, but the
fees alone – beyond the obvious help to
publicise the book – are hysterical. I hope
you're aware how much the Greta craze

has taken hold. I have little girls (and not a few boys too) outside the office with their parents dressed in their homemade woollen forcefield hats trying to meet you. Sales, as I hope Jonti explained in his email with the revised contracts for the rest of the trilogy, are, frankly, unprecedented. I don't think I've ever seen anything like this happen so quickly.

I'm sure it has already occurred to you, but there will come a point when you will need to give an interview face to face. Emailed Q and As and quick phone interviews are great, but the honest truth is, either we do it ourselves, controlling the atmosphere, and with some influence over the tone, or some hack will track you down and knock on your door anyway. If you could have a think at least, that would be great. If not, of course I will do what I can to keep the 'mystique' alive!

Love to the family,

H xxx

Sent from my iPad

B   Dear Harry,

I'm so excited that everyone seems to have taken Greta so firmly to their hearts. Thank you for forwarding all the letters, some are so cute! They really make me feel like I am sharing something with so many people and that they, if this doesn't sound too grand, understand and like a little part of my mind. It's a wonderful feeling.

I would really appreciate it if you could continue to refuse interview and appearance requests. With Caroline and how I'm feeling I would rather keep everything normal as much as I can. Even going online to read reviews is a bit much for me. Can the PR team keep up the 'reclusive writer' angle until I recover? Frankly it seems like sales have a good momentum all on their own, I wonder how much they need a helping hand from me!

I hope you understand,

H

A   Hi Heather,

I hope you are feeling better. Everyone at the office is tremendously excited as the launch of book two approaches. Parker have just signed on to make commemorative pens! Not sure yet whether they'll be able to shoot out magic fire, though! ;)

I just wanted to say personally how excited I am that you'll be able to attend the launch event. We have come so far! People are so desperate to meet you! You deserve to feel the warmth of the embrace of your public!

Plus, I am looking forward to giving you a big hug and telling you with all my heart that working on your books has been the apotheosis of my professional life.

With love,

Harry.

PS. Attached are the revised contracts for the video game: Greta now won't be able to hold a gun, a knife, or any weapon other than the pen.

B

Dear Harry,

Thank you so much for your kind and heartfelt words. I'm so excited about the launch too and I hope it goes without saying how grateful I am to you and all the team for all the hard work you've done and are doing. You've believed in me and Greta since the beginning and I'll never forget that.

Unfortunately I have some bad news about the event. I dearly, dearly wish I could join you all for the launch but I'm afraid I must again disappoint you. I've taken a turn for the worse I'm afraid and found out this morning that I have to begin some treatment in a few weeks time that my doctor tells me will be pretty heavy. I implored him to let me travel down but he said he couldn't promise it would not have a negative effect on my health and of course I can't take any risks. I have to think of Caroline.

I know this will be a disappointment to everyone, but please be assured that it won't be half as disappointing as it is to me. I'm gutted.

Yours,

Heather

A
Dear Heather,

I'm heartbroken. I've been trying to ring you but can't get through. I have told the team and, though I don't want to speak too soon, we are making plans to try to move the whole launch up to you. A street party outside your house if need be. I don't want to get your hopes up (it will cost a lot more and it's a logistical nightmare) but the early signs are looking good. Pam even thinks it could be a great selling point and frankly there is so much interest in you and the book that I think the press would happily do the junket in a nuclear waste facility if there were signed copies and free egg sandwiches.

Give me a call to discuss.

Love,

H

B
Oh Harry please don't go to all this trouble, I don't deserve it. I beg you not to move the event. I'm ill and I look terrible and I feel worse and I couldn't manage it. Really I can't manage it. Harry I implore you as a friend, please don't make me feel worse than I already do.

Do the event in London. Let it be a success. Let people read the books and I will get on with writing the third.

H

A
My dear Heather, the last thing I want to do is upset you. I have been trying to keep you

away from this as much as possible but after your last email about the launch, the hype surrounding the second book, the first film about to come out, there is just too much interest in you. It is too big a story.

I wish I could hold them off, I really do, but I am increasingly worried that the price on your head is too great.

The rumours on the internet, if you haven't seen them yourself, range from insulting to macabre. Only this week someone sent me this link to a *Buzzfeed* article called *10 similarities between Heather Eames and Father Christmas*. Number eight is 'only children think they exist'.

I wish I could give you better news but this is the truth my darling: they will find you. And when they do we can't control them. If we take control now, do a short appearance at the launch, then *Piers Morgan's Life Stories* or something, that will be the end of it and you, Caroline and Ian can go back to living in peace.

Lots of love,

H

B   Dear Harry,

Thank you for being straight with me. I'm afraid you're right. I'm afraid they will find me eventually. I'm afraid once they do they might not like me.

That's just it you see… I'm afraid.

Could we not do more phone interviews?
Or I could write another, longer
autobiographical piece for a newspaper?

Thank you for trying to help, you're a dear
friend,

Heather

A   Heather, what are you afraid of? What on
           earth is there not to like? Do you think the
           British public want some stuck up angel
           whose arsehole smells of talcum powder?

           Don't be ridiculous! They want *you*. Exactly
           as you are. They want to tell you how
           much they love Greta! They want to share
           that love with you! They couldn't give a
           rat's arse if you have three heads and a
           moustache like Hitler on each one.

           H

B   Harry you're hilarious.

           I hope you're right. I suppose I am worried
           what they will make of me. I'm not what
           they expect you see. Although my arsehole
           does smell of talcum powder. Xx

A   What is it my dear? I promise you, it will
           be so so so much better than you think.
           Think what we have been through together
           Heather – you can trust me.

           H xx

A   Please Heather, whatever it is, share it with
           me. I beg you.

           H

A	Heather? Are you getting these? There's no answer on your phone and I haven't had a reply. Please darling, tell me what's on your mind.
B	Dear Harry,
	I lied to you. I don't have a daughter.
	I'm sorry,
	Heather
A	Dear Heather,
	Is that it! That's the secret you're afraid of! Honestly, Lord Byron was a sex-addict with a pet bear, I think people will forgive you a little fib.
	What did I tell you – there's absolutely nothing to worry about! Shall I arrange a cosy interview where you can explain to people why you felt you needed to lie?
	Xx
B	I don't have a husband. And I don't have cancer.
A	Ok. Like I said Heather, the British public have forgiven far, far worse than a bit of lying. It might be a bit rough for a week or two but there's nothing people like better than a redemption story. I promise, everything is going to be ok. You have created something wonderful.
B	I'm in prison.
A	What?

B	My name isn't Heather Eames. This is just an email address I made. My name is Tariq Medjani.
	I am sorry to have deceived you like this. I felt that a name like Heather Eames would be a better fit for the story. I don't know why. It was stupid.
A	Why are you in prison?
	Why are you in prison?
	If you don't tell me it will be impossible to control.
B	I killed three people.
A	No email in response.
B	I'm sorry Harry.
A	No email in response.
B	I was afraid. But I want to be honest now.
A	I need some time to think about this. I need to have a think about how to deal with this.
B	Two of them were children. I'm sorry Harry.
A	I need to think about this. Please just give me an afternoon to think about this. To work out a strategy. I need to talk to Pam and the PR team.
B	It was a mother and her children. They were a family.
A	Please Heather. I need to think. Please.
B	When it happened I was in a very dark place. I don't have an explanation but I was

not well. Sometimes my mind would go to a place that was not me and I was unable to control it.

A   No email in response.

B   I followed her home after I saw her coming out of Pizza Express on Hendon Way. I pushed her through the door as she let herself in. I was someone else.

I made love to her in the corridor.

Her children woke up and came downstairs.

They were panicking. I panicked.

I cut their throats open and then their mother's.

That's the truth. I'm sorry Harry.

2. CONVERSATION

B	My house! My family!
A	I know.
B	My front door is covered in graffiti.
A	I know.
B	My house. My kids. My fami my fucking family I have two daughters and they are being bullied. Bullied.
A	What
B	They are six and eight.
A	do you want?
B	Six and fucking eight.
A	I'm sorry.
B	My Aston. My fucking Aston smashed up!
A	I know.
B	So when you sit there and you say why are you here this is why I'm fucking here this is why this. To tell you. To fucking to tell you.
A	Yes.
B	To see you.
A	Ok.
B	To
	Silence.
A	It's ok.
B	I should smash your
	Silence.

145

B	I should.
A	I know.
	Silence.
B	And this coffee tastes like shit.
	Silence.
B	And this is what you look like.
A	I'm sorry Harry.
B	Sort of what I imagined. Like sort of what I had in my head what I thought it would be.
A	Really I
B	Like what you wrote to me about when you saw the Greta film. It's what was in your head but at the same time something different.
A	The film.
B	And as soon as you see the real version the one you had in your head dies a little bit.
A	I couldn't watch to the end.
B	Just like I imagined. Tall.
A	Yes.
B	Strong.
A	Yes.
B	Male.
	Beat.
B	Dark hair. Less hair than I imagined.

A	Thanks for noticing.
B	More tattoos.
A	Hm.
B	More scars.
A	Yeh.
B	Fuck.

Silence.

B	Seriously fuck you.

Silence.

B	Fuck. Fucking. Fuck you. I should sm

Silence.

B	I didn't used to imagine you like that obviously. I used to think you were, you know, five two, mousy brown hair, reading glasses, wonky teeth.
A	Yes. Well.

Beat.

A	For what it's worth
B	Mm?
A	You're going to laugh.
B	I doubt it.
A	I thought you were a man.
B	What?
A	All this time I thought, I don't know why, I assumed 'Harry'.

B	
A	But here you are. Blonde bob. Pale skin. Expensive suit.
B	Thanks for noticing.
A	The guards probably think you're my wife. One of those pen pal–
B	What's that?
A	Nothing.
B	Jesus it's bad. You've been beaten up?
A	It's fine. It's normal.
B	They want money?
A	I guess. It's ok. I've got money.

Silence.

B	Jesus this really does taste of shit.
A	You should try the food.
B	God help me.

Silence.

B	Tariq Medjani.
A	Yes.
B	Why didn't you tell me the truth?
A	Come on.
B	Why didn't
A	You know the first word I wrote
B	You just
A	Of the very first book?

148

Pause.

A   I read an interview with JK Rowling about how she came up with Harry Potter, you know. How she was on a train looking out the window and suddenly she saw all these wizards flying outside the window. How she was seeing these witches and wizards flying around and suddenly she realised that this boy Harry was sitting on the train. Like imagining it was actually him looking out of the window. Where was he going? What was he going to do? And suddenly she saw it all as clear as if they were all already written: the magic school, the arch enemy the whole fucking thing laid out.

B   So what was it? You were cutting some kid's throat and you thought, shit this would be a great chapter in a story about pre-pubescent witches?

A   Heather.

B   What?

A   Heather was the first word I wrote. I didn't have anything. No Greta, no Scorax, no Pen of the Necromancer, no story, no Code of the Ancient Witches. Nothing. I just wrote that word. H. E. A. T. H. E. R. And I thought, what comes next? What's lovely? What is the loveliest name in the world? Eames. Heather Eames. And then I was on the fucking train. I could see it all.

B   Scorax, Greta, the witches–

A	No. No that was all later. I could see Heather's house. I could see her husband. I could feel him inside me as they tried to have a baby – they'd been trying so long. I could feel her cancer growing, starting to corrupt her and kill her.
B	Jesus.
A	She had to finish the story quickly because I knew she was dying. She was dying as soon as she was born. She's the saddest character in the whole book.
B	And it just happened to sound, I don't know, female, white, English?
A	I gave the people what they want.
B	No.
A	Jaqueline Wilson, Gayle Forman, John Green. The biggest kids writers.
B	You underestimate people.
A	Jeff Kinney. Joanna Rowling. Are you beginning to notice something?
B	You killed a family. That's not prejudice, that's a fact.
A	And you think if it had been Heather, if it had been 'Heather Eames' who had killed that family
B	What are you
A	You think the people the papers you think the world would have had the same reaction being told that Heather Eames was a killer?

B	The name isn't important.
A	Or John Green or Jesse Andrews?
B	People reacted to the facts.
A	The facts are my name! My name changes the facts. And if you don't believe me then that's then you don't know

Silence.

B	Heather Eames. It's a lovely name.

Silence.

A	I want to show you something.

Tariq puts onto the table a thick pile of printed pages. It's the manuscript for the final Greta book.

B	Tariq.
A	I know what you're going to say I've heard it but please just think about it.
B	I.
A	Look at it.

Harry sighs.

A	Hold it.

Harry picks up the manuscript. It's the most beautiful woman she's ever seen. It's a work of art. It's a bar of gold.

B	'Greta and the Cave of Shadows'.
A	Good title eh?
B	Harry Potter rip off.
A	Fuck you.

She turns to the first page.

B   Greta and the Cave of Shadows. By Heather
            Eames.

Silence. She turns another page.

B   Darkness had fallen right across the world,
            from the icy plains of the north to the
            southern deserts. It was midnight, and alone
            in her father's study at number 15B Acorn
            Street, sat a young girl, short for her age
            and with a dark brown ponytail that fell
            halfway down her back. She was staring
            at something in her hand. A small object,
            glittering in the light from her father's desk
            lamp. It was the pen he had given her
            before he died. The pen that only a few
            years ago she had

She stops reading. She catches her breath.

B   Jesus. I don't want to stop.

A   It's good Harry. I promise you it's good.

B   It's not about being good.

A   Put it out as someone else. Say you had
            it ghost written by primary school kids in
            deprived areas.

B   Tariq.

A   We'll give all the money to charity.

B   Look

A   We'll. We'll. Please.

Silence.

B	Our revenues are down nearly 20%.
A	I'm sorry.
B	It's not as much as we expected.

Pause.

A	People are still buying it.

Pause.

B	My office was picketed.
A	I'm sorry.
B	I've had death threats.
A	I know.
B	I've had to leave Twitter.
A	I can't
B	My daughters, my fucking daughters get bullied
A	I'm sorry Harry.

Silence.

B	They want to know what happens though.
A	Yeah?
B	Jesus the youngest can't sleep without her Greta doll.

Silence.

A	They were good weren't they?
B	Tariq.
A	They were though. They were fucking good.
B	Don't.

A	Its just, I haven't read the first two for a while so. Sometimes I do, you know, they let me have them sometimes. They're not always like I remember. It's funny. Like I wrote them they came out of this out of me but I still don't really know them like I can still be surprised.
B	They're not yours anymore.
A	Yeah.
B	They're their own thing.
A	It's the first time we see Scorax that always gets me. I always remember it differently and then when I read it I'm like ah. Yeah that makes sense, that's so much better.
B	I love that bit.
A	How did I do that the first time if I can't even think like that now?
B	It's a wonderful moment.
A	It's like it wasn't even my head, like it just came from someone else, dropped in.
B	Michaelangelo said that the sculpture was already in the marble, he just had to uncover it.
A	Bit pretentious.
B	I suppose.
	Silence.
B	For me it's when Greta first finds the pen. The description of it 'glinting like a wolf's eyes in the window'.

Silence.

B   You're a monster.

Pause.

A   Yes.

B   You are an evil evil wicked man.

A   I know.

B   You have done unspeakable things, caused unspeakable turmoil.

A   I was ill. I am

B   Horrible.

A   Ill

B   Horrible. Just horrible things.

Silence.

B   And then.

A   I know.

B   And then this.

A   I am ill.

B   Where did it *come* from?

A   I know.

B   How did you do it? Do both. How did you do both?

A   Release. I don't know. Release from something. Escape.

B   God.

A   From something.

B	They are so beautiful Tariq.
A	Yes.
B	So so beautiful. When I read them to my girls for the first time. When I heard their breaths draw in as Greta found the pen. When I felt their hearts flutter as she stepped through the curtains and into Rossini's Clock Shop. You gave that to me. You were there with us, the two of us together reading telling that story in my daughters' bedroom in my
A	I'm sorry
B	God in my daughters'
A	I know.
B	Sitting on the bottom bunk.
A	It is beautiful.
B	Inside my house.
	Silence.
B	Horrible.
A	Why didn't you insist?
B	I beg your pardon?
A	Please, I'm a bit ill, I've just had a baby. You knew that if you came to visit me you would find something you didn't like. It was better for you just to have the manuscript and hope that everything else went away.

B	I begged you to do a book tour. I sent endless invitations to the launch, to do interviews.
A	Whatever.
B	I phoned you. I thought I was speaking to you remember. Chatting shit to your sister in law. Some fucking housewife in Mill Hill.
A	You liked the story as much as I did. The middle aged woman
B	I hope you paid her I hope she got a slice.
A	Rejected by everyone else
B	Bullshit.
A	Until one genius editor a knight in shining armour
B	I was busy. I have a company to run. I can't just drop everything to go and have lunch with some pregnant first time writer just cos she can't be fucked to come down to see me.
A	Right.
B	It doesn't mean I thought she was a fucking serial killer.
A	I'm not a serial killer, they all happened on the same night, it was one incident.
B	For fuck's sake.
A	Shit like that matters ok at least describe it accurately. You're supposed to be a fucking editor.

Silence.

A	How many writers do you represent?
B	I don't know, fifty maybe.
A	And how many haven't you met?
	Pause.
B	None.
	Silence. Harry looks again at the manuscript.
A	It's the same story Harry.
B	Is it?
A	This doesn't change the story.
	Pause. Harry shakes her head. She can't.
A	I've taken up embroidery.
B	What?
A	Yeah they run this class in here, it's called Knitting Behind Bars. A woman comes in, Lynn, and teaches us how to knit and sew and stuff.
B	They let you have knitting needles?
A	We make these she calls them Comfort Dolls. They're like I don't know like little teddy bears I guess little woollen dolls.
B	And then what?
A	I think she puts them on her blog. People buy them. The money goes to community groups and stuff.
B	Don't Tariq.

A	People do lots of people buy them. It's about rehabilitation. People like to think
B	Tariq
A	Think that there is recovery you know people want to have
B	I can't have this
A	Hope
B	Conversation
A	People believe in redemption.
B	Only people who don't know what you did!
	Pause.
B	People buy a doll from a prisoner. Of course they do. That's because in their mind he's a misunderstood poor boy who got mixed up in a bad crowd and ended up shooting a drug dealer.
A	That's not
B	People buy these dolls because they can just make up their own criminal. You think someone will buy a children's book from a man who raped and killed a mother and her children?
A	I.
B	Tariq.
A	That wasn't me.
B	I'm sorry.
A	That wasn't.

Silence.

B   The Lego's been pulled.

A   That's a pity.

B   You'll still get paid.

A   What about the theme park?

Pause.

A   I am Heather. I still am.

B   Tariq.

A   Greta saved me.

B   I don't care. I can't care.

A   If you spoke to Lynn, you'd see, the Knitting Behind Bars it

B   It

A   Works, people care.

B   doesn't matter.

Pause.

B   It doesn't matter.

Harry holds the manuscript.

B   They were my daughters' age.

A   I can't I don't know

B   They could have been my little girls.

Harry holds the manuscript.

B   This will be the last time you see me.

A   Yes.

B	We'll still pay your royalties of course.
A	Thanks.
B	I'm sorry Tariq. I'm sorry things turned out this way.
A	Don't be. I am what I am. I've done what I've done.
B	Yes.
A	Good and bad.
B	Yes. Good and bad.

Harry holds the manuscript. She can't stop looking at it. Silence.

A	People will buy it Harry.
B	Yes.
A	It's the end of the story. People care what happens.
B	Yes.

Pause.

B	I've been talking to Warner Brothers. They want to go ahead with the third film. Do it in two parts you know.
A	People want to know how it ends.
B	Yes.
A	They want to know if Greta's safe. They want to know if she turns out ok.
B	Yes.
A	Harry?

Harry looks at Tariq.

A   That's why you came today isn't it?

B   Yes.

3. SCREENPLAY

A	EXT. THE MOUNTAINS OF THE NORTH
B	Helicopter shot of the mountains. They are cold, unforgiving and barren. The clouds rumble with the coming storm, obliterating the moon.
A	EXT. THE CAVE OF SHADOWS
B	In the centre of the mountain range, unmistakably jutting from the skyline is the largest mountain of them all.
A	As we wheel around it we notice that the deep crevices in the rock make up a pattern. It is unmistakable: hewn into the surface of the rock is the face of Scorax, her features contorted. Her mouth open.
B	This is the Cave of Shadows.
A	INT. THE CAVE OF SHADOWS
B	Darkness. The cave is illuminated only by the flashes of lightning from the raging storm outside.
	The walls are etched deeply with runes and old spells. Bad things have happened here.
A	CRASH.
B	A sound from the edge of the cave and GRETA pulls her top half onto the edge of the cave.
	Greta looks BATTERED and BRUISED. On her cheek is the still-bleeding wound from the Night Ravens. Her hair is tied up and her eyes are steeled.

A	GRETA: (under her breath) Come on, Greta. Come on.
B	With her last ounce of strength Greta hauls herself up onto the ledge, and collapses, breathing heavily.
	ECHOING CACKLES fill the room, then disappear.
A	Greta tenses, frightened, then grits her teeth. She's got to do this.
B	She pulls herself to her feet and as she does so we see some rubble from the cave floor FALL out of the mouth of the cave and into the night. Greta watches it fall and fall and fall until it disappears into the darkness.
A	Greta gulps.
B	In her hand she clutches the PEN OF THE NECROMANCER.
A	GRETA (CONT'D): T-O-R-C-H.
B	The pen SHOOTS out a shaft of brilliant LIGHT, illuminating the walls of the cave.
A	Greta GASPS.
B	Across every wall are etchings, carvings, runes and spells.
	As she approaches with the torch the runes and carvings begin to MOVE like SNAKES across the wall. She sees snatches of words: REGRET, HURT, PAIN.
	GRETA:

A	Sandy was right: the carvings move. That's why the graffiti on Ben's bedroom door had disappeared by the time we arrived.
B	Suddenly there is a SCREAM from somewhere inside the cave. Greta wheels round.
A	Ben?! Ben, I'm coming!
B	But before she can move there's a:
A	BOOM!
B	The wall bursts apart.
A	Greta stumbles backwards and then
B	S-H-I-E-L-D!
A	A shield grows from the pen as debris and shards of rock fly past Greta's head.
	BANG!
	A large rock crashes against the shield and knocks her to the floor, then... silence.
B	Rnnng.
A	She looks up and sees that her leg is trapped underneath a pile of rocks.
	Suddenly, there is the sound of SCREEECHING. High and horrible, it echoes through the cave and sends a shiver down Greta's spine.
	Greta strains to see a shadow moving along the sides of the cave. It's coming towards her.

	The shadow is high and thin and long. And at the end of one of its arms is a thin-fingered, bony hand holding... a pen!
B	No. No! NO!
A	A foot appears on top of the pile of rocks. Then a leg. Then all of a sudden, standing on top of the rocks at Greta's feet is the tall, towering figure of...
	SCORAX, her red eyes glowing in the blackness.
B	GRETA: It's you.
A	SCORAX: Yes. Are you surprised?
B	I don't understand, you're...?
A	Dead?
B	I saw you die. I saw you fall from the Cliffs of the Burning Moons.
A	That's true Greta. But did you see me land?
B	Wh-?
A	Did you see my body break?
B	No.
A	Did you see my head sink below the waves?
B	No.
A	Did you hear me cry for help or beg forgiveness?
B	You know I didn't.
A	Then how did you know I was dead?
B	I–?

A	You should know better than anyone Greta that death is not that simple. Ever since the first time we met, in the corridors of Rossini's Clock Shop, you've known. I live, Greta, because I live in you. I exist because I exist in you. Do you think it's a coincidence that I have a pen like yours Greta? Do you think it's a coincidence that we first met the day after your father died? The day you inherited the Pen of the Necromancer. Greta, I am your... SHADOW!
B	No! That's impossible! I'm nothing like you. I'm...
A	Good?
B	Greta stares at her. This can't be true. She's good. Isn't she?
A	We FLASH into her thoughts:
B	Greta's POV as she
	– STEALS the potion from McKlusky's desk.
	– BLASTS the Necromancer from the Thousand Mile Ridge
	– LIES to Ben and Sandy about finding the emerald pin.
A	END FLASH. Greta gasps. It can't be. I've tried to be good.
B	Answer me this, then, you feeble, worthless worm: who was there the day you couldn't stop Ricardo falling from Harlow's Tower?

A	You.
B	Who was in your nightmare the morning before you betrayed Lord Scree?
A	You!
B	And whose shadow did you think you saw just before Ben disappeared?
A	But – how could you be in all those places at once? How could you change shape so quickly?
B	Well that's easy. The answer… is in your hand.
A	Greta looks to her hand. And in it, clutched in her fist, is her PEN.

My pen.

B	You never found out where it came from, did you Greta?
A	I…?
B	Your pen was carved from the tusk of the last Snow Stag. The Snow Stag was a beautiful creature. Its pelt was soft as January snow. It's eyes, dark and red as dying fire. The last of its kind was just a fawn. No bigger than a lamb it was and before it died it was hunted for days, right across the North. When it was killed its blood stained the whiteness of the snow in which it lay and its hunter took his prize. The great tusk of the beast, more magical and valuable than anything before or since. And from that tusk he carved–

A	A pen!
B	No Greta. He carved… two! Your pen has a dark twin. Hewn from the same father, housed in the same bone, my pen and yours are intertwined. You see Greta you think that you are Good and I am Evil but I'm afraid it's not that simple. I AM you. You ARE me.
A	No! B-O-L-T!
B	A lightning bolt shoots from the pen and EXPLODES the pile of rocks. Greta rolls free of the rocks that trapped her. Scorax has been blasted to the other side of the cave.
A	The two enemies scrabble to their feet and face each other across the cave with their pens out.
B	What do you want?
A	I want the second Pen of the Necromancer.
B	Why?
A	You have no idea of the force you wield in your hand. All these years you've been using it to conjure silly spells and children's magic tricks. To write little stories for your friends that make you feel *safe* and *happy* and stop you being scared of the dark – never knowing its true power.
B	What do you mean?
A	You really are so young Greta.
B	What can it do?

A	So young and so green.
B	Tell me!
A	The two pens bestow on their master the most precious power of all. The power to…
B	What?
A	Talk to the dead!
B	ZZZING! A bolt of lightning flies forth from Scorax's pen.
A	FFSHAA! A whoosh of air flies from Greta's.
B	The two witches are blown into the air by the power of the mutual blast. The two spells interlock and twist together.
A	The walls of the cave blow red, then blue, then green with the magic of the combined power.
B	Greta and Scorax are raised up by the spell and drawn together.
A	They are pulled closer and closer.
B	What's happening?!
A	Give me the pen Greta.
B	No.
A	Give me the pen!
B	The spell has overtaken them now,
A	They can't control it, but are within it, without it, like atoms in a galactic burst.
B	Their bodies are drawn together. The walls of the cave flex and stretch.

A	The words in the rock glow gold and black and burst with fire. There is another BLAST and Scorax and Greta are pinned next to each other onto the floor of the cave.
B	They look up at the starburst of spells coming from the two pens, now discarded and floating in the air, humming and vibrating from the power of the magic. They are both terrified.
A	Still staring up at the starburst, their hands, almost without thinking, reach for each other
B	and CLASP together.
A	SCORAX: I can't control it.
B	GRETA: I'm afraid.
A	Me too. I'm afraid too.
B	The light between the two pens glows
A	and bends
B	and begins to take shape. It is a small dot at first.
A	Then the dot becomes a circle.
B	Then the circle splits into two.
A	And the circles become eggs.
B	And the eggs stretch and grow until they are shapes they both recognise.
A	GRETA: You were right.
B	SCORAX: Yes.

A	GRETA: The dead.
B	The light is now two bodies. The bodies of two children, shimmering like liquid silver.
A	Children?
B	Yes.
A	Where is their mother?
B	I don't know.
A	Are they alive?
B	I-I don't know. This is deep magic. Old magic. I can't control it.
A	The pens – look!
B	The pens are floating above the outstretched palms of the two children. SCORAX: This is the prophecy of the Necromancer: the two pens will raise the dead to tell their story together.
A	FLASH! Fire flows from the pens and surrounds the children.
B	It jolts their bodies stiff. Slowly, incrementally, their mouths open.
A	And their mouths are as deep and as black as night.
A and **B**	There is a place. South even of the Cliffs of the Burning Moons. It is a place of infinite beauty, where the waves kiss the shore like a mother to her children. Where the sun nurses the forest so that it grows green and strong and vast. We love you. We love both of you. It's ok. It will be ok. We forgive you.

INSTRUCTIONS FOR CORRECT ASSEMBLY

Instructions For Correct Assembly was first performed at the Royal Court Jerwood Theatre Downstairs on 7th April 2018 and featured the following cast and creative team:

MAX	Jane Horrocks
HARI	Mark Bonnar
JÅN / NICK	Brian Vernel
LAURIE	Michele Austin
PAUL	Jason Barnett
AMY	Shaniqua Okwok

Directed by	Hamish Pirie
Designed by	Cai Dyfan
Lighting by	Jack Knowles
Music by	Duramaney Kamara
Sound by	Helen Skiera
Movement by	Vicki Manderson

Characters

MAX, *around 50*
HARI, *around 50*
JÅN / **NICK**, *18-20*
LAURIE, *around 50*
PAUL, *around 50*
AMY, *18*

Place

The rooms of a neat family home. It could almost be a catalogue.

A note on Jån and Nick

In my mind Nick and Jån are played by the same actor, so to all intents and purposes are identical. As a result at times there may be a tension, even confusion, about who we are watching.

1

Kitchen

MAX	Did you find what you were looking for?
HARI	Yes I did. Lovely girl helped me in the shop. She pointed me in the right direction.
MAX	Oh good.
HARI	On the way out I noticed they had a special offer. A do it yourself type thing.
MAX	You like those.
HARI	Exactly. It's not much of a commitment financially speaking and might be a bit of fun.
MAX	Sounds good.
HARI	I thought we could have a go at it together, you know like we did with the upstairs bed?
MAX	Oh I enjoyed that.
HARI	You had natural flat pack talent.
MAX	You said I was the Susan Boyle of DIY.
HARI	This might be a little more complicated than the bed but still, I'm sure it's the kind of thing we can crack on our own.
MAX	Is it in the hall then or
HARI	No. It contains some special components or something so they send it out direct.
MAX	Well I'll look forward to that.

Garage

HARI and MAX stand surrounded by parts. A chaos of bits and pieces. HARI is looking at a page in an inch-thick book of instructions. MAX is trying to peek at it too. They read intently, very confused.

MAX	Can I have a
HARI	One second.
	Silence.
MAX	Just a quick look
HARI	One second love stop breaking my concentration.

Silence. HARI peers at the book as if the distance he's reading it from will make a difference. MAX opens her mouth to speak. Then closes it. Silence.

HARI holds the book out for her to take. She takes it. She turns to the first page.

MAX	One: check you have all of the component parts. Two: take the laminate frame (left) and place it on its plastic neoprene base, upright. Twist two of the fiddly ones into the pre-drilled holes in the heel.
HARI	These?
MAX	Yes. Two. Attach the toe mouldings to the tops of the fiddly ones and screw.
HARI	What do you mean the top?
MAX	The top. I'm just trying to describe the drawing.
	He does it. It looks good.
MAX	Hey how about that.

HARI   Well that's the beauty of it. It's all these separate
              parts. They come in bits. They're scattered
              all over the floor. You're looking at them and
              thinking okay this doesn't make any sense
              how will this ever fit together and be our new
              bed or desk or whatnot and I wouldn't have
              thought that that went there or in that order but
              then two hours later once it's all come together
              you're looking at it and thinking: wow.

Study

HARI is on the phone.

HARI   Well I'm struggling to see why I pay for next
              day delivery if it's not guaranteed. Yes that's the
              whole reason I signed up for the prime service.
              Yes also for the ad-free access to the premium
              music library and the original video content.
              I've started season one but I didn't get into it if
              I'm honest. Did you think? I thought it was a
              bit too complex for its own good actually. Yes
              sort of never bought into the concei– Look this
              is totally off the subject. I paid for something
              perfect. I don't think it's too much to ask to be
              delivered something perfect. There are some
              missing components and I need them sent out
              as soon as possible. Some ball bearings, some
              stainless steel six pins. And well I've got a list:
              Ball bearings, chrome, 5; Six pins, stainless
              steel, 2; Circuit board, 1; Glass eye, grey-green,
              1; Wig, Chestnut, 1; Toenails, 3, left big, right
              third, right pinky; Last one, lithium batteries.

              Pause.

Thank you.

Garage

HARI and MAX are surrounded by parts, working to fit two pieces of plastic together.

MAX	I have to say I think it's very clever all these things. I mean it's a faff putting it all together and when you lose a bit and the staff can be annoying but when it works it is very good.
HARI	I think they're an excellent company.
MAX	What they've done is take the real expense of the work
HARI	The manpower
MAX	Out of the equation
HARI	Exactly
MAX	And said, okay, here's all the stuff, but wouldn't you rather do it yourself than have some guy in a factory
HARI	Who's more expensive
MAX	Who's more expensive anyway
HARI	Or in a factory in India or something
MAX	Which is immoral and gone well go on then off you go have a good Sunday and give us a call if you get stuck.
HARI	Which you're very welcome to do.
MAX	Like we did with the wardrobe.
HARI	Yes although that was their fault.

MAX	Why because you put the drawers in upside down?
HARI	The instructions were vague.
	They continue to work.
MAX	I had an email from Jenny. They're all visiting Fi in Hong Kong.
HARI	Gap year?
MAX	Yes she's got an internship apparently. She said over 400 people applied.
HARI	Wow. Clever girl.
MAX	Yes. Have you got the Phillips?
HARI	Toolbox.
MAX	And did you see Jeanette reposted an article her son wrote for a magazine which looks very good.
HARI	Gosh he's done well if he's writing for a magazine.
MAX	I'd not heard of it before but Jeanette's post said you can get it in shops you know it's not just online.
HARI	Impressive.
	They are making progress.
MAX	Hey you'll never guess who just did my eyes at the hospital.
HARI	Dr. Safani wasn't there?
MAX	No there was a junior doctor. Milo Hooper.
HARI	You're kidding. He can't be old enough to drive.

MAX	He still looks about twelve.
HARI	So he's a doctor?
MAX	I know.
HARI	I remember when he and Nick got suspended together.
MAX	And Jill gave me hell as if it was my fault.
HARI	I'll say now what I said at the time: if he wasn't involved then why was he holding the can of Lynx.
	Pause.
HARI	A doctor.
MAX	I know.
HARI	Wow.
	Pause.
HARI	Good on him.
MAX	Absolutely.
HARI	Jill must be chuffed.

MAX nods. She holds up what she's been working on: it looks like the perfect plastic arm of a male manikin. They look at each other. And smile.

Living Room

HARI stands opposite JÅN, a boy of about eighteen.

Silence.

He stares at JÅN, who stares back, impassive.

HARI	Well?

Silence.

HARI   Are you going to say something?

Pause.

HARI   Anything?

Pause.

HARI   Great.

                HARI leaves the room. JÅN stands in silence.

                *HARI returns carrying a toolbox. He removes a
                screwdriver from the toolbox. He goes to JÅN. He
                unscrews the back of JÅN's head and removes it. He
                presses something. He pulls out a cluster of wires and
                circuitry. He finds a particular wire and looks at it. He
                sighs. He cuts the wire. He replaces the back of JÅN's
                head. He stands back from him again and presses a
                button on a shiny remote control.*

JÅN   Hello.

HARI   That's better.

Conservatory

HARI, MAX, PAUL and LAURIE are having a pre-dinner drink.

LAURIE   We honestly couldn't believe it. Paul picked
                up the phone and as soon as I heard her
                voice I thought: this is going to be good news.
                Whenever she has bad news she waits for us
                to call. Or worse, we get a call from Minty,
                that's Ames's best friend – absolutely brilliant
                painter actually we went to one of her shows
                last term and she really is exceptionally talented
                – anyway she'll call and it's all oh Laurie there's

                                185

been a disaster, we've missed the last train can
you come and pick us up from some nightclub
or other we've been having too good a time.
Anyway this time it's Ames on the phone and
I just grabbed it off Paul – I wasn't going to let
him have all the fun – he got the AS's, I got
the GCSE's so it was my turn – and bless her:
she was crying. Tears of joy. Three A stars and
an A, and to be honest I think the chemistry
department is total rubbish at that school so at
any normal school I think it might even have
been four A stars. So she's off to Oxford at the
end of the month.

HARI   To Amy!

Dining Room

HARI, MAX, PAUL and LAURIE are in the middle of dinner.

PAUL   You wouldn't believe the amount of work
they have to do. I mean I try not to get too
involved but I had to have a word with the
coach I said Phil these are fourteen year old
kids, you know, they've got homework, they've
got social lives, Callum has this girl he's trying
to lose his virginity to – oh come on I'm only
joking – but you take my point, they can't be in
every morning at six smashing lengths before
school. It's taking the joy out of it. Cal used to
love swimming, he'd take it seriously of course,
you have to if you're at his level, but he used to
do it because he enjoyed it. With these national
squads it's just work work work; they treat them
like they're professional athletes. I said come on

Phil give him the weekend off let him go on this
date or whatever. And you know what he said
to me he said: when Callum's got an Olympic
medal round his neck, he'll have all the pussy
he wants.

They all laugh.

HARI   To Callum!

Sitting Room

HARI, MAX, PAUL and LAURIE are having an after-dinner coffee.

LAURIE   I'm actually genuinely concerned. Paul will
               tell you that I've been having trouble sleeping
               because of it. Tossing and turning and just
               trying to think how best to handle it. I mean,
               what kind of pressure does it put on a child
               to be told you're an actual genuine prodigy?
               At architecture. At eleven years old. I mean
               how can they know? Of course these tests are
               evaluated by RIBA so it's all legit but still, when
               her form teacher's looking me in the eye and
               saying that in twenty years time Sophia will be
               the next Zaha Hadid what are you supposed to
               say?

MAX   It's fucking ridiculous.

HARI   To Sophia!

Kitchen

MAX and LAURIE are clearing up.

LAURIE   Ames sends her love by the way.

MAX   Oh that's kind send it back.

LAURIE   She was so upset she couldn't get down for the funeral.

MAX   Oh god I didn't even think about it.

LAURIE   It was just you know because she'd already been signed up and it was abroad you know not just a day trip or whatever and I think it counted towards her coursework so.

MAX   Honestly I wouldn't have wanted her to cancel. It's great she's so focussed.

LAURIE   She said she'd sent a card?

MAX   Yes. It was very sweet.

LAURIE   Well that's good that's polite.

MAX nods. They wash.

LAURIE   Also because it was booked through the school I think that was another reason they couldn't cancel it or something. I just don't want you to think that she was being rude.

MAX   No, I don't.

They wash a bit. Silence.

LAURIE   And how are you both doing?

MAX   We're good. We're good.

LAURIE   Good.

They wash.

MAX	It can happen to anyone that's what's so terrifying.
LAURIE	Of course it can.
	Pause.
MAX	It's not anything you've done or that anyone's done it's just
LAURIE	No quite quite.
MAX	You know Amy or Callum or Sophia. You know?
LAURIE	Mm.
MAX	Could have been.
LAURIE	Mm could have been.
MAX	It's just well you just don't know.
LAURIE	No.
MAX	No.
LAURIE	No.
MAX	No.
LAURIE	No.
	They wash up.
LAURIE	That lamb was really terrific by the way. You put me to shame.

Garage

PAUL and HARI are admiring JÅN.

HARI	You can touch him if you like.

PAUL approaches and begins to have a root around.

HARI   The really clever thing it does actually come
        here you'll like this. If you want to tell it a story
        about yourself, you know some goal you once
        scored or thing you did that was really cool.
        Well if you programme it right he'll remember
        all that stuff and upload it to the cloud so you've
        got a sort of walking sort of legacy.

PAUL   Sweet.

HARI   Of course they're a bit more unreliable the
        flatpack ones

PAUL   That's the price you pay

HARI   But I invested a little extra to get a call out
        helpline so if anything does go wrong – simple.

PAUL   Speaking of money, Hari.

HARI   Have a feel here. I mean you expect a little
        give and take around the jointing but this is
        practically invisible. Go on have a real feel.

PAUL strokes JÅN's face.

PAUL   Ooh yeah. That is lovely. What's the traction
        control like?

HARI   Oh he'll go anywhere – alright Paul. *(PAUL
        stops stroking.)* We haven't done it yet but I've
        seen a tutorial on YouTube take him mountain
        climbing.

PAUL   Get out.

HARI   Seriously. He's got PLS palm grip, and Double
        Knuckle Cladding on every finger so should
        be able to hold on to just about anything you
        throw at him.

PAUL's got his head to JÅN's chest.

PAUL	Nice growly base notes coming from there.
HARI	Oh there's some pretty serious punch under the hood.
PAUL	You know from this angle it almost reminds me of
HARI	It's just one of the standard appearance packages actually.
PAUL	Has a similar sort of
HARI	I think there are a couple of ones you can go for.
PAUL	No. No right. (*Looks at the packet*) Oh yes I can see here, Selected Finish: "White and Polite".
HARI	The truth is most of this is just casing. The real processing power's on a chip that sticks to the back here look.
PAUL	Quite versatile then.
HARI	Oh completely. In theory with a good scalpel and some anaesthetic there's no real reason you couldn't fit it to a I don't know a cat.
PAUL	Maybe I'll fit one to the wife. Might be the only way I can get her to tidy her tennis stuff away! And what you train him up do you? Try to give him a grounded moral framework based on viewing your actions and the actions of people within his environment from which he begins to interpret the social norms of the locale in which he's been placed?
HARI	Yup. I'm also doing quite a lot with the remote control.

PAUL	And dare I approach the thorny issue of cost?
HARI	I mean it's an outlay of course it is. But once you're paying monthly and you think about the premium nature of the product and what it can do. Really not that bad at all.
PAUL	Speaking of money, Hari
HARI	The height's generous.
PAUL	Just would be good to have a chat about
HARI	Good options on eye and hair colour.
PAUL	You know not rushing just to get an idea of
HARI	Yeah no of course. I've spoken to the bank. I should have the bulk with you by the end of the year.
PAUL	Great.
HARI	We really do appreciate it so much.
PAUL	I know you do. That's not why I'm
HARI	No I know
PAUL	It's just cos we're saving up for the loft so

Pause.

PAUL	Poor Nick.
HARI	Yeah.

Silence. They look at JÁN again.

PAUL	So when do we get a chance to meet him?

Kitchen

MAX	When?

HARI	The fourteenth. Here let me do all this you made dinner.
MAX	Oh Hari.
HARI	What was I supposed to do he was interested?
MAX	It's just pressure that's all. I don't want
HARI	What they're our friends!
MAX	I know but
HARI	There that's on eco-wash – done by the time we wake up.
MAX	We haven't even met him ourselves yet.
HARI	They just want to come round and see him. He'll impress them. Believe me.
MAX	*(Imploring.)* Please. What if he's embarrassing or we can't get him to behave or
HARI	Oh come on it doesn't matter. They'll just come round, meet him, be impressed, then leave, what's so scary about that?
MAX	Please Hari. I'd just rather not.
	Pause. HARI sighs.
HARI	Alright. I'll text Paul and make an excuse.
MAX	Thank you.

Hallway

HARI	Cab's here!
NICK	*(Off)* Coming!
	NICK enters. He looks identical to JĀN.

MAX	Got everything?
NICK	Yes Mum.
HARI	Need a hand with anything?
NICK	I think I'm good. See you guys.
HARI	'See you guys' listen to him as if he's popping to the shops.
NICK	I'm gonna see you in a few weeks. It's not a big deal, is it?
MAX	Er our big grown up boy is going to university and one day he's going to be a big grown up man and time goes past very quickly and I'm your soppy old mum so yes it's a big deal!
NICK	Alright alright.
HARI	You look very smart mate.
NICK	Cheers Dad.
MAX	You've got your bag?
NICK	Er no I thought I might actually leave my bag.
HARI	I see you've packed your cheek.
MAX	What would he do without it?
NICK	Guys I've got to go.
MUM	You've got your admissions letter.
NICK	Mum it's online you don't need to bring it.
HARI	Passport?
NICK	Dad
HARI	Careful with your passport
MAX and NICK	"It's the most valuable thing you own"

HARI	It is! And remember when you get your room – first thing you check?
NICK	That the shelves have been put up right.
MAX	Hari what kind of
HARI	It happened to a friend of mine in our first term. Bang, knocked out cold by an Oxford Dictionary of Quotations.
NICK	Sorry Mum.
MAX	Sorry for what?
NICK	That I'm leaving you alone with him, you going to be okay?
HARI	*(Cuffing him playfully.)* Maybe you should leave some of that cheek at home eh?
MAX	So you'll call us when you get settled in won't you?
NICK	Course.
MAX	And you're definitely going to try to quit smoking?
NICK	Mum.
HARI	Good luck mate – knock 'em dead.
NICK	Will do.
	He picks up his bags.
NICK	Well
MAX	Well
NICK	Gis a hug then.

2

Garage

MAX is reading from the instructions. HARI is fiddling with JÅN who is inanimate.

HARI   Read it out for me.

MAX   Okay. So. In order to setup an SD card with a newly built version of SON you will need to: 1. Format the selected SON persona into the / output as BORN. 2. Copy onto

HARI   Hang on hang on. And. There.

JÅN wakes up, enthusiastically.

JÅN   Don't tell me this is my room? Honey I love it! OMG it's literally perfect I'm like having a literal heart attack right now. The poured concrete, the garage doors, the full sized car accessory it's like 'mechanic-chic' or something, it's gorgeous, it's cheeky.

MAX   Maybe turn down the 'opinionated' dial?

JÅN   Did you guys do this damp wall? It is out of this world I'm going crazy here!

HARI   Definitely.

HARI fiddles with something on the back of JÅN's head.

JÅN   I love how you've just like scattered shammy cloths everywhere. Seriously it's like you've taken a Pinterest of like my dream room and just like built it.

HARI   Okay let's try this!

HARI presses something.

JÅN   Oh. My. Days. Is this my room?

HARI	Oops, I think I turned it the wrong way.
JÅN	Bitch what was you thinking? These walls are like puke coloured or some shit. What you walked into Homebase and was like here give me a paint that looks like I done a shit on a hangover.
MAX	Come on Hari.
HARI	Right you are. Ah, I think I've found the Sassy guage. I'll just take it right down shall I?
JÅN	And I'm sorry yeah but this door fuck me are you cunts blind or something?!
MAX	Right down.
HARI	Here we go.

JÅN switches to a meekness bordering on psycopathic.

MAX	Jån?

JÅN looks at MAX.

MAX	Jån?
JÅN	*(Monotone.)* You have pretty eyes.
MAX	Er, okay.

JÅN looks MAX up and down, studying every inch of the skin on her face.

JÅN	And your skin is lovely.
HARI	I might just split the difference.
MAX	Do.
JÅN	Could I see your teeth?

HARI makes another change and JÅN switches to a confident, polite, eighteen-year-old boy.

JÅN	Hi.
MAX	That looks better.
JÅN	Is this where I'll be sleeping? It's nice.
MAX	Much better.
JÅN	It's great to finally meet you both properly.
	They look at him, and smile.

TV Room

HARI and MAX are refitting parts of JÅN. His body parts are in pieces around the room. His head rests on the side. The TV is on and they half-watch as they work. HARI is screwing some circuitry in a leg. MAX begins to cut down the flesh of an arm, consulting the instructions at all times.

HARI	Have you seen the left shin?
MAX	It's round here somewhere.
HARI	I was polishing it earlier before I had a go on his nostrils.
MAX	Is this it?
HARI	That's a buttock, Max.
MAX	Oh.
HARI	Honestly we'll end up with the bloody elephant man with you in charge.
MAX	I knew we shouldn't have done it inside.
HARI	I wanted to watch out for Katherine she's supposed to be in this one.
MAX	Sort of could be a shin.

HARI	Ah here we are; in with the toes and feet. I thought I said
MAX	Sorry sorry
HARI	I'm not having a go but otherwise things'll get lost and you only notice you're missing a piece when it's too la – ooh ooh!
MAX	Is that her?
HARI	Yes.
MAX	No.
HARI	Yes!
MAX	Gosh she's grown up.
HARI	Wow.
MAX	She's very good.
HARI	Intense!
MAX	Yes.
HARI	Sexy!
MAX	Alright Hari.
HARI	Sorry.
MAX	Ooh watch out Katherine I don't like the look of that storage room one bit.
HARI	Haven't you been reading the papers there's a bloody killer on the loose?
MAX	Well don't go in on your own.
HARI	You sexy idiot! Ah!
MAX	Eurgh!

They watch her get killed. A pause for breath.

HARI   Very good. She was always talented.

MAX   I should text Fran and say we saw her.

HARI takes the shin over and begins screwing it into the knee. They work a little in silence.

MAX   You know – you'll think I'm soppy – but, sometimes, I think my favourite times with Nick were just those, were just you know those schoolnights not doing anything. Like we could go on holiday or maybe out for a meal for someone's birthday and it was lovely of course it was but somehow, I don't know, it *had* to be lovely if that makes sense? Whereas some nights, when the three of us were just, maybe, like this, watching TV together, the kind of night you'll forget about ninety-nine times out of a hundred. But we'd be all sitting there and just, watching you know and, yeah, I don't know, you'd be half-reading the newspaper, Nick'd be texting or on whatsapp or whatever the latest thing is or doodling a tattoo on his arm and yeah it was just nice, you know?

Pause.

MAX   Have you got an elbow lying around by any chance?

HARI   Oh sorry yes, I was using it as a paperweight.

Dining Room

MAX, HARI and JÅN are eating dinner. JÅN is playing with his food. MAX nods at HARI and HARI taps JÅN on the shoulder. JÅN stops playing with his food.

MAX	Shall we tell our days?
HARI	Oh yes.
MAX	Jån?
JÅN	Yes please.
HARI	Right I'll go. I went to school. Had a good day actually. Got some jip from year 13 but had a nice lunch. I popped round to Al's on the way home too, which was nice. He said I could help myself to his old washing machine if I fancied it. I thought I might take the motor out and have a fiddle around. I'm sure there'd be some good parts in there. Max?
MAX	I had a lovely day. I met Carla before work which was really nice. She's thinking of going back to work, now all the kids are at school.
HARI	That's a good idea.
MAX	Work was good. They're trying to get me to train up the new boy in Kitchenware so he can take off some of my workload which will be excellent.
HARI	It's not fair the way they work you.
MAX	So hopefully this can be a way of getting some of my life back. Then I went to yoga and had a really good sweat.
HARI	We're eating love.

MAX	How about you Jån? What did you do?
JÅN	*(Talking with his mouth open and full of food.)* I cleaned my room.
HARI	Jån?
JÅN	Sorry. *(Still open and still full of food.)* I cleaned my room thoroughly.
	MAX and HARI look at each other. MAX nods. HARI takes out the remote and taps on it a few times. Beep!
MAX	What did you do again Jån?
	He swallows the food, but mumbles monosyllabically into his chest with his head down like a sulky teenager.
JÅN	Clned m'room.
HARI	It's okay it's okay.
	HARI fiddles with the remote again and nods at MAX.
MAX	Jån?
	JÅN now talks eagerly and clearly looking each of them in the eye in turn.
JÅN	I cleaned my room from top to bottom, it took ages but was worth it as now I have everything just the way I like it.
MAX	Good boy. What else?
JÅN	I ate a nice lunch.
MAX	What did you have for lunch?
JÅN	I had a sandwich of bread and cheese and swimming.
	Beat.
HARI	Again.

JÅN	A sandwich of bread and cheese and swimming.
HARI	Of bread?
JÅN	And swimming swimming.

MAX and HARI glance at each other.

JÅN	Swimming swimming swimming swimming swimming.

HARI gets up and fiddles with the back of JÅN's head. He returns to his seat and taps on the remote.

HARI	Again.
JÅN	A sandwich of bread and cheese and ham.
MAX	Yum yum.
JÅN	Then I watched some television. A comedy show about some hilarious poofs who

HARI taps the remote. Beep.

JÅN	A comedy show about some hilarious queer

Beep.

JÅN	About some hilarious gay

Beep.

JÅN	Some hilarious people. It was really good. I liked it because they smack each other over the head the whole time and there's a guy in it who always ends up with his face in the mud. It makes me laugh so much.

Pause. MAX nods. HARI fiddles again.

JÅN	I like the show so much because the people in it are so stupid they're always doing stupid things.

Pause. HARI fiddles again.

JÅN	I don't really like the show though. I think the way it portrays the characters is patronising to be honest.
MAX	In what way?
JÅN	They have no opinions of their own. They just fall over or get banged on the head and stuff. It's supposed to be funny.
MAX	Well it sounds a bit silly to me.
JÅN	Then I made myself a cup of tea.
MAX	Mmmmm.
JÅN	A really fucking strong one. Not that grey milky shit Max sometimes slops up.
	Beep.
JÅN	A nice strong one, much better than Max's.
	Beep.
JÅN	But I couldn't get it quite how Max does it unfortunately.
MAX	Practice makes perfect.
JÅN	I'll have to keep a better eye on you!
MAX	Haha exactly.
HARI	It's nice to just put your feet up with a cup of tea sometimes isn't it?
JÅN	Fuck yeah! *(Beep.)* Hell yes! *(Beep.)* When you feel it's well earned.
HARI	Quite.
JÅN	I took the tea outside I hope you don't mind.
MAX	Of course – it's your house too.

JÅN	Just into the conservatory. It's nice being amongst all the flowers.
HARI	Isn't it.
MAX	A little piece of heaven I sometimes think.
JÅN	There's no such thing as heaven.
	HARI pauses over the remote. He and MAX have a look at each other. They let it go.
JÅN	And I sat with my tea and had a read of the paper on Hari's computer. Hope you don't mind Hari.
HARI	Anything interesting?
JÅN	Some stuff about immigration. Everyone seems up in arms one way or the other.
HARI	It's a complex problem.
JÅN	Dunno, seems simple enough to me. England should stay English what's so complex about that? There are parts of Birmingham that have Erdu street signs.
HARI	Well
	Beep.
JÅN	I just think the middle class totally disregard the genuine fear of the working man that lower paid jobs are being taken by cheaper immigrant workers and traditional white working class communities are being broken up.
	Beep.
JÅN	All international borders are illogical constructs that have more to do with a self-perpetuating

oligarchy of rich capitalists than any actual
concern for culture or the welfare of the people.

Beep.

JÅN The way the papers twist the immigration issue
is, to be honest, offensive. Modern Britain is
multicultural, that's what makes us who we are,
that's what makes us successful. Look at Mo
Farah. If we didn't allow skilled immigrants
into the country the NHS for one would totally
collapse and that's supposed to be our crown
jewel.

MAX Look at nursing.

JÅN Exactly, the nursing profession is propped up
by skilled immigrant workers.

HARI Not to mention art, culture

JÅN The whole idea of traditional Britishness is
fake anyway, we've always been a tapestry of
influences.

MAX I couldn't agree more.

JÅN Anyway then I got bored of the paper so I went
on the internet and had an incredible wank
to some really filthy stuff I found *(Beep.)* To a
google image search of Katy Perry. *(Beep.)* Did
some homework in my room for half an hour.
An essay about the objectification of women in
the modern media.

MAX Sounds like a very productive day.

JÅN Then I went outside for a bit.

MAX Oh.

HARI Hmm.

MAX	I'm not sure how we feel about that.
JÅN	Just down to the corner shop.
MAX	Right?
JÅN	I bought a packet of fags. Came back here and had them in the garden. They were lovely; really moreish. Ended up just smoking one after the other.

MAX and HARI look at each other. Beep. JÅN goes to sleep. Silence.

HARI	Getting there.
MAX	Yes.
HARI	I'll have a look in the instructions about those cigarettes. Just a bit of rewiring needed I expect.

Pause.

HARI	This is delicious by the way.

Kitchen

NICK	So
HARI	Hi.
NICK	Hi.
HARI	Your mum's in bed.
NICK	Well it's late so.
HARI	Yeah.

Silence.

HARI	Do you want anything? A cup of tea? Or I could warm you something up. We had some

	lasagne, there's some lasagne in the fridge if you fancy.
NICK	I'm good. I ate at the station.
HARI	Great. Yeah some good options at the station. There's a Pret I think even now did you see that I mean I know you know that's probably not your

Silence.

HARI	Anyway.

Pause.

HARI	I won't wake Mum if you don't mind. She's been having trouble sleeping anyway so.
NICK	It's fine.
HARI	You can see her in the morning.
NICK	Yeah.

Silence.

HARI	How've you been?
NICK	How've I been?
HARI	Have you been staying with friends or?
NICK	Friends.
HARI	We've not heard from you that's all
NICK	Sorry.
HARI	It's been three weeks so we were getting a bit
NICK	Were you?
HARI	Of course.

Silence.

HARI	It's good to see you.
NICK	Yeah it's good to see you too.
	Pause.
HARI	You sure you don't want
NICK	I'd have a beer if you've got one.
HARI	A beer. Yeah sure why not? I'll join you. Why not have a beer?
NICK	We don't have to.
HARI	No a beer's alright isn't it?
	He gets two cans.
NICK	Thanks.
	Silence.
NICK	So
	Silence.
NICK	I've been having a
	Silence.
HARI	This is nice isn't it. Got it wholesale at Costco actually so it works out pretty good.
	Silence.
NICK	I was wondering if I could borrow a bit of money.
	Silence.
HARI	I thought we said
NICK	I know
HARI	Cos we did lend you for your pop-up café
NICK	I know but that wasn't my fault

HARI	And then when you needed to visit your girlfriend in Dublin after her
NICK	I know
HARI	And then for your TEFL course.
NICK	Yeah. It's fine.
	Pause.
HARI	It's not like we have loads of cash just swimming around.
NICK	I know.
HARI	So you'll be okay?
NICK	Of course.
	Silence.
NICK	I should push off.
HARI	What?
NICK	I should get going.
HARI	But you're not staying?
NICK	I can't.
HARI	You've not seen Mum.
NICK	Tell her I said hi.
HARI	Nick
NICK	I'm staying with a friend so
HARI	You're welcome to stay here.
NICK	Nah.
HARI	Stay here for a few days just shake yourself off a bit.
NICK	I'm fine.

HARI	We can spend some time together Mum would love to see
NICK	I can't.
	Pause. HARI nods. NICK goes to the door.
HARI	Nick. Here take this at least okay. Just use it to get something to eat or.
NICK	Pret?
HARI	You will though yeah?
NICK	Of course.

Garage

They are polishing JÅN's parts. His head, separated from the rest of his body, rests on its own, but is animate.

MAX	We were thinking Jån that
JÅN	Yes?
HARI	Oh bloody hell.
MAX	Well wondering really
HARI	I've lost the belly button again.
MAX	Oh Hari.
JÅN	You were thinking what?
	Beat. MAX and HARI look at each other. Big news.
MAX	That if you wanted you needn't stay
HARI	Only if you fancy a change
MAX	Yes only if you fancy
JÅN	Spit it out Max.

HARI	You needn't stay here in the garage.
MAX	We thought you could come into the house. Take the spare room.
HARI	It just feels a bit cold out here and well you're part of the family now aren't you?
MAX	It's only going spare anyway so
HARI	Ah here it is! *(Fishes it out of his pocket.)* Confused it with a 20p piece!
JÅN	I'd love that.
HARI	You would?
MAX	Then it's settled.

3

Basement

HARI	Now she's off!
JÅN	Look at her go!
HARI	Toot toot!
JÅN	I'd say we'll have the coal delivered before sundown at this rate.
HARI	Sundown? She'll be there by tea! Easy now bring her down a bit careful not to overheat the engine. That's it nice and steady. There. Now we just let her fly.
JÅN	Round and round.
BOTH	Toot toot!
	They watch it go.
JÅN	How long have you been into train sets?
HARI	God ages. Love the engineering side you know.
JÅN	Oh it's not a toy.
HARI	No quite.
JÅN	They're extraordinarily detailed aren't they all the models. Did you paint them yourself?
HARI	No they come painted.
JÅN	Still you fit them together really well.
HARI	Yes I do like the composition of the landscape. I fancy myself as a bit of a designer when it comes to this.
JÅN	I think I could really get into it myself.
	Silence. The train whizzes round.
JÅN	What's this piece?

215

HARI	Oh that's old doesn't actually go with this set. Different sized tracks. Leave it there.
JÅN	There's loads here.
HARI	Yes I bought quite a lot of it at one point never quite took off. Don't worry about it.
JÅN	It's a bit bigger than this. Is it for kids or something?
HARI	Yes. Yes it's for kids.
JÅN	Barely been touched. This clock tower's not even been opened.
HARI	No. Hey come and have a look here I'm about to change the signals.

JÅN returns. Silence as the train loops and loops.

HARI looks at JÅN. JÅN nods. HARI offers him the controller. JÅN takes it, but leaves his hands there holding HARI's. Silence.

HARI	You know
JÅN	Yes?
HARI	Here's a thought. Maybe you're just humouring me but
JÅN	What?
HARI	Well you might not be interested but. Never mind.
JÅN	Please.
HARI	I was going to say that if you like the look of that unused set feel free to help yourself.
JÅN	What?
HARI	You can have it if you like.

216

JÅN	I?
HARI	Be good to see it go to a good home.
	Pause.
JÅN	I'm going to play with it every day.

Garden

MAX	Peonies.
JÅN	Peonies.
MAX	Roses.
JÅN	Roses.
MAX	Daffodils.
JÅN	Why do they call them daffodils?
MAX	I don't know. It's a nice name though isn't it?
JÅN	It's lovely.
MAX	These are foxgloves. They grow wild if you're not careful.
JÅN	I like learning about the flowers with you Max. It's nice.
	Silence. They busy themselves arranging the flowers.
MAX	Jån.
JÅN	Yes?
MAX	You don't. You don't need to call me Max if you don't want. I mean you can but. I'd like. I'd like you to start calling me Mum. Would you do that?
JÅN	Alright then.

MAX	Thank you. That means a lot to me.

He smiles, and keeps working.

MAX	You have to prune the leaves to keep them all thriving.
JÅN	It's hard work.
MAX	It can be but the satisfaction is enormous. Just think when we're done we can enjoy the garden.
JÅN	Come out here and read.
MAX	Yes.
JÅN	Or have some friends over for a glass of wine.
MAX	Lovely idea.
JÅN	Or just come out here in the evening and take in the air.
MAX	My thoughts exactly.
JÅN	I could definitely get used to it. Oh stay still.
MAX	What is it?
JÅN	Here. A ladybird it was in your hair.
MAX	What a delicate little thing.
JÅN	It's beautiful.
MAX	Yes.

They watch it crawl on JÅN's finger.

MAX	Can I ask you something Jån?
JÅN	Of course.
MAX	What's it like in in in your I mean what's it like for you to.

JÅN	To?
MAX	I suppose I'm saying do you ever get things in your head and you just can't you can't shake them?
JÅN	Oh. Erm. I don't think so. For me everything seems to move in straight lines.
MAX	Straight lines.
	JÅN smiles.
JÅN	Hey.
MAX	What, another?
JÅN	No it's
MAX	I'm sorry
JÅN	A little tear.
MAX	I think it's the pollen.
JÅN	It's okay.
MAX	The hayfever. I should probably go inside.
JÅN	No. Come on let's stay out here a bit longer. It's so nice, Mum.
	Pause.
MAX	Yes. Alright then.
	They watch the ladybird crawl along JÅN's finger.

Study

Night. Silence. On the desk is a camera, its little charging light glowing red.

The window slides open and NICK crawls through, looking worse than ever. He stands still for a second, taking in the room.

The door opens and HARI comes in. NICK has made for the window but stops.

HARI	What the – hey – what the
NICK	Shhhhh
HARI	Nick?!
NICK	Please shhhh
HARI	Nick what the hell are you
NICK	Please
HARI	Scared me half to death surprising me like that what were you thi
NICK	Shhh Dad please don't shout
HARI	How on earth did you get up here?
NICK	Please I just wanted to
HARI	I thought it was a burglar I thought I was gonna get burgled or raped or
NICK	Dad
HARI	Or
NICK	*Dad*
HARI	Christ.

Pause. HARI calms down.

HARI	God what is that? Oh Nick you – you stink.
NICK	Sorry.
HARI	Where have you been? You don't look you look terrible.
NICK	Alright.

HARI	You should have called first
NICK	I know
	Silence.
HARI	What's that?
NICK	It's nothing. A scratch.
HARI	From a ruddy tiger you've been beaten up.
NICK	Don't worry about it.
HARI	But I do. That's the thing. I do.
	Silence.
NICK	You look well.
	Silence.
NICK	Nice bookshelves.
HARI	Thank you, they were doing a deal on them so.
	Silence.
NICK	Is that new?
HARI	Huh?
	They look at the camera.
HARI	Yes. Mum got it for me.
	Silence.
HARI	No Nick.
NICK	No what?
HARI	You're going to rob your own house.
	Pause.
HARI	You're breaking into your own house to
NICK	Nobody's perfect Dad.

HARI	I'll call the police.
NICK	No.
HARI	I will I'll I'll call the police. And I'll wake Mum.
	Pause.
NICK	I'm sorry Dad.
	Silence.
HARI	You're going to die Nick.
NICK	Yeah. Well.
HARI	I wish you wouldn't. I wish you'd just I wish you'd just not left. I wish you'd just stayed in here with us and we'd kept on and you hadn't been
NICK	But I am.
HARI	I know.
NICK	That's how I am.
HARI	Yes but.
	NICK approaches the camera. They look at each other. He picks it up. HARI doesn't say anything. NICK goes to the window.
HARI	It's my birthday. You know that? It's my birthday today.
NICK	Yeah.
HARI	Is that why you came back?

Living Room

MAX	You have to Hari

JÅN	Give it a go
HARI	No I'm crap!
MAX	We're all crap that's why it's funny!
JÅN	Go on Hari we've all had a go
HARI	Alright alright bloody hell it's like being back at school here okay get ready with the timer
JÅN	Dun da da da
MAX	Ladies and gentlemen!
HARI	None of that come on let's just get on with it!
JÅN	Three. Two. One. Action.

HARI starts a mime. He's really crap. MAX and JÅN start cracking up.

MAX	Toad?

HARI shakes his head.

JÅN	Frog?

HARI shakes his head.

JÅN	Toad in the hole?

HARI shakes his head.

MAX	Toadstool.
HARI	It's nothing to do with bloody toads alright!
JÅN	Nananana!
MAX	Don't speak!

He continues. He really is terrible.

JÅN	What kind of thing is it?
HARI	It's a film.

MAX	Mime it don't say it!
JÅN	Have you ever played this game before?
	Does the mime.
HARI	Film.
	He keeps miming it.
MAX	How many words?
JÅN	Three words.
MAX	Whole thing.
JÅN	Angry.
MAX	Angry man.
JÅN	Fat man.
HARI	Steady on.
	MAX and JÅN are really laughing now.
MAX	Killer!
JÅN	The Devil Wears Prada?
MAX	Where did that come from?
JÅN	Kill Bill?
MAX	Dead.
JÅN	Shoot. Shooting. Killing. Shoot.
MAX	Time.
JÅN	Good Will Hunting!
HARI	Yes!
	They all collapse in giggles.

TV Room

MAX and HARI are watching TV with JÅN. HARI is half-heartedly reading the paper. The silence between them is easy, contented. After a while JÅN begins idly doodling a tattoo on his forearm.

MAX looks around the room at her family, who continue with their little preoccupations.

HARI looks up and they catch each other's eyes.

They smile. Silence.

At length, HARI reaches for the remote and presses a button.

Kitchen

NICK is sitting at the table. He looks better than when we last saw him. He's getting better. In fact with his upright posture, his relaxed breathing, and the way he gently smiles at MAX as she potters about the kitchen we might almost think it's JÅN.

NICK	I really like this kitchen.
MAX	You do?
NICK	Yeah. I forgot how much I liked it. I like the plants in the window and the toaster in the corner. I like the light coming through from the garden. I like I really like being back here.
MAX	Well we like having you back.
NICK	My flat's not like this I'm afraid.
MAX	No. No it's not like this.
NICK	It's not a nice home.
MAX	No.

NICK	This is a nice home. No one would prefer that home to this one would they?
MAX	Well you can stay as long as you like.
	Pause.
MAX	I tell you what. Why don't you sit there and I'll toast you a bagel.
NICK	Okay.
	She starts working in silence.
NICK	How have you kept this!
MAX	What? Oh I like it!
NICK	Mum I did this when I was like five.
MAX	It's sweet!
NICK	Why have I done the house in purple?
MAX	I think you'd run out of red.
NICK	Come to that why is Dad green!?
MAX	Haha – I like the way the sun is sort of staring at us like –
NICK	Ha! He looks like some sort of sex pest!
	They laugh at the drawing. Pause.
NICK	I'm gonna do it this time Mum.
	She looks at him.
NICK	I can feel it. This is the one. I want you to know that. It's not that I don't want to be better, I do. I do. I do. That's all I want. I know I've let you down and that I'm probably the worst son in the world. I don't want to be, I really don't. I want to stay here to stay here and be clean and

live with you guys. I really really really really really really want that.

She nods.

MAX   Good. Because you know Nicky, there is nothing nothing I would like more than that.

          Silence.

MAX   Now how about that bagel?

Kitchen

HARI, MAX, LAURIE, PAUL, AMY and NICK sit at the table having brunch.

LAURIE   Mm these are delicious Hari, wow aren't these good Ames?

AMY   Fantastic.

HARI   Oh well Nick helped as it happens.

NICK   I cracked the eggs.

          Everyone laughs.

MAX   No no but he did more than that, you did more than that Nick, don't do yourself down.

HARI   Yes Nick was, what do they call it on Masterchef, Nick was my Sous Chef!

PAUL   Very good.

MAX   So how's school Amy?

AMY   Not bad thanks.

HARI   Your A-levels must be coming up.

AMY   Yeah we just had our mocks.

LAURIE	Amy was pulling her hair out with stress. Honestly in our day we were allowed to mess up play around have a second chance. For her you know because she's got that offer from Oxford she really has no margin for error so it's just pressure pressure pressure.
AMY	Thanks Mum.
LAURIE	No but you know what I mean.
HARI	Well congratulations on your offer Amy, that's that's really something to be very proud of well done. Even if you don't get the grades now you know at least you've had the offer.
NICK	Dad.
HARI	What no I don't mean it like that I mean.
MAX	Oh Hari.
HARI	She knows what I mean. I'm sure you'll get the grades I'm just saying. Ignore me.
AMY	Haha it's okay Hari I know what you meant. To be honest I'm really not that stressed about it. I think I might even prefer to go to Bristol anyway.
PAUL	A lot of her friends are going to Bristol so.
LAURIE	How are you Nick, how's the café?
PAUL	Hari told us you were trying to start up a little café?
NICK	Oh, yeah, well it was more of a sort of food van thing to be honest like for festivals and stuff.
PAUL	Ah okay and?

NICK   It was good but getting into all the good
          festivals was really hard cos I think they've
          been working with all the same people for years
          and don't want anyone new so.

          Silence.

LAURIE   Well it's great that you gave it a go.

PAUL   I think it's a good thing. Bill Gates dropped
          out of uni didn't he? Country needs more
          entrepreneurs. The best idea is the next idea
          know what I mean?

          Pause.

LAURIE   Or if you've got a passion for cooking you
          could try getting some experience in a
          restaurant first. You know build up your
          knowledge base then branch out on your own.

NICK   To be honest it was more of a way to get into
          festivals but yeah that is a good idea.

          Pause.

PAUL   So it's music you're into then? Well you're still
          young, you should start your own band. Hey
          what was that band Hari that started in your
          school?

HARI   Coldplay.

PAUL   That's it see everyone's got to start somewhere.

AMY   Coldplay started at Bart's?

HARI   Well one of them went there. The drummer I
          think.

LAURIE   Start a band now, practise hard, you could be
          playing those festivals in few years.

229

NICK	I don't know. I'm not that good at music to be honest. Just like listening to it I guess.
	Silence.
MAX	Nick's doing really well. We're really proud of him, aren't we Hari?
HARI	Yeah. Dead proud.
NICK	Thanks guys.
MAX	He's been through a lot but he's on the home straight.
LAURIE	Of course he is.
PAUL	To Nick! *(They all toast.)* Listen Nick. This might not be of any interest to you but, if you like, when you feel ready, you're very welcome to come and have a few shifts at the shop?
NICK	Really?
HARI	Seriously Paul? That's very kind.
PAUL	He'd be doing me a favour – we're always looking for good new people.
LAURIE	Only to tide you over you know until you want to go back to college maybe or apply for a course or
PAUL	Oh it's not a job for life – just a bit of pocket money.
MAX	What do you say Nick?
	NICK is truly touched. He nods, choked up.
NICK	I'd. I'd really like. Thanks Paul.

HARI	You better watch out though, he'll be running the bloody company in a few years and might fire your lazy arse!
PAUL	Haha fine by me I could do with a bit more time with my good friend Mr. Nine Iron.
LAURIE	It's so lovely what you've done with this room Hari I think it every time I come round.
HARI	So much lighter isn't it? I did all the joining myself as it happens. Why pay someone good money for something you can teach yourself on YouTube?

As the others talk, MAX and NICK share a warm smile. She reaches and squeezes him affectionately on the arm. He smiles.

Teenage Boy's Bedroom

Evening. NICK is sitting alone.

He gets up and picks his phone off the desk. He returns to the bed and swipes through some things, then puts it down.

He opens his laptop, and idly checks some things, glancing at his phone as well but, bored, gives up on that too. He closes the computer. He drops the phone on the bed.

He goes to the window and looks out.

He steps away from the window and takes a deep breath.

He goes back to the window and opens it. The sounds from the suburban street outside drift in. He leans out of the window and breathes it in.

He comes back into the room and steps away from the window again.

He freezes. He shakes his head. He knows.

He takes a backpack from under the bed and puts his laptop in it. He puts his phone in his pocket.

He goes back to the window and climbs out, feet first, until only his torso is visible, preparing to shimmy down the drainpipe.

The door opens, and MAX comes in carefully holding a mug of hot chocolate.

MAX	I thought you might like

She sees NICK, his body half out the window. They look at each other. Pause.

NICK	I'm just going to meet Amy. She said some of her friends were getting together so.

Pause.

NICK	I'll be back in an hour.

They look at each other.

MAX	Please. Nick please.

A pause. And then, he goes.

MAX stands in the empty room, looking at the empty window.

Conservatory

MAX stands in the empty room, looking at the window.

MAX	Hari!

HARI enters.

MAX	I've changed my mind. I think we should have Laurie and Paul round to meet Jån.
HARI	I thought you said
MAX	I said I've changed my mind Hari is it *that* fucking hard to understand?
	Beat.
HARI	I'll send them an email.

4

Attic

HARI is staring at JÅN, glass-eyed. MAX has fallen asleep.

JÅN   Nothing gives me more pleasure than a
            good book don't you agree? The themes the
            characters the feeling of wholesomeness one
            gets from simply getting lost in good words and
            what *(Beep.)* I was thinking tomorrow we could
            maybe go into town and see if we can find that
            Diesel Shunter you were talking abou *(Beep.)*
            Okay okay I'll go first. Um, alright got one:
            Vegetab *(Beep.)* And if I just shift this finger then
            that's offsp *(Beep.)* There *(Beep.)* How *(Beep.)*
            Some *(Beep.)* You're the best.

            Pause.

JÅN   I really mean that. The best Dad in the world.

            HARI looks at MAX, checking she's asleep. Beep.

JÅN   This may sound a bit disloyal but

HARI   It's alright. What's on your mind?

JÅN   I just feel like, having thought about everything
            that happened, you know with Nick that.

HARI   What?

JÅN   Well if Max had just listened to you, you know,
            if she'd been a little more patient.

HARI   A little more trusting I suppose you could say.

JÅN   Then maybe I don't know maybe things would
            have turned out differently.

HARI   My point of view was simply that nothing
            is beyond repair. Take the stuff up here for
            example. This fax machine. A lot of people

	might give up the ghost. Might think of it as junk. But my point of view is – always has been – that with a bit of perseverance you can always find a use for anything.
JÅN	Nothing should be just… thrown away.
HARI	I tried to explain that to her. I tried but she wouldn't listen. She insisted Jån she said if he ever came back we had to turn him away. Do you believe that? Turn him awa
	MAX stirs. HARI notices, quietening down. Then, after he's sure MAX has settled again – beep.
JÅN	If she'd only listened to you.

Airing Cupboard

MAX and JÅN iron and fold. MAX hasn't slept in days.

JÅN	Do I have to perform?
MAX	Of course not, you just need to
JÅN	To?
MAX	Be the engaged, polite personality you always are. I just want them to meet you, simple as that.
JÅN	I can see why you like ironing. Getting everything flat and fresh and folded away.
MAX	Hari even likes his underwear done, can you imagine?
	They smile.
JÅN	Doesn't Laurie go on and on about Amy. I mean Jesus it gets to the point where you're

	like alright already I get it we all love Amy but enough.
MAX	It's not her fault. She doesn't know what it's like to to have to deal with.
JÅN	I'm just saying it's all been so easy for her.
MAX	She's had an easy ride of it that's what Hari says.
JÅN	If she had been through what you and Hari had
MAX	Well
JÅN	God you'd see that facade crack soon enough don't you think?
MAX	I don't know. I wouldn't wish it on
JÅN	Imagine her trying to cope with what the two of you
MAX	Yes. Maybe.
JÅN	And what makes it worse is that silent judgement.

MAX reaches for the remote control. Beep. Pause.

JÅN	What makes it worse is that smug little bitchy judgement face.
MAX	You mustn't say things like that Jån.
JÅN	If I were you sometimes I'd wish Nick had got Amy involved too then she'd see.

Beep.

| JÅN | Sometimes I'd wish it had been Amy not Nick. |

Beep.

JÅN   Sometimes I'd wish Nick had gone out with
            Amy and that he'd fucked her stupid perfect
            little brains out.

            Beeep. He holds up a pair of beautifully ironed y-fronts.

JÅN   How's that?

MAX   Perfect.

Attic

NICK   I've got some news. I know I've been away
            for a bit and you were probably worried and I
            can totally understand why. I'm sorry I haven't
            been in touch but I didn't want to get your
            hopes up and then let you down again because
            I know I've done that too many times already.
            I've been getting myself straightened out. It's
            been hard work it's been really hard work but
            I did it. I'm better now. I don't expect you to
            trust me or even to like me much at first, but I
            came here today to promise you that even if it
            takes the rest of my life I'm going to show you
            that I'm better.

            HARI looks at MAX, she's welling up. She nods.

HARI   You don't need to apologise darling. We forgive
            you. Do you want to come and stay here for a
            bit? I could get the Dyson out and have your
            room spick and span in no time.

NICK   Thanks but, I've actually got my own place.

MAX   Your own place.

NICK   Yeah. Like I said I didn't want to get your
            hopes up so I didn't tell you but, once I felt

better I started looking for work. I ended up taking Paul up on his offer. I begged him not to say anything because I didn't want to let you down if I couldn't handle it. I really enjoyed it, keeping inventories, managing stock. After a while Paul and Laurie were so impressed they asked me to take over from Monique when she left to have a baby.

HARI   Isn't she the store manager?

NICK smiles.

NICK   Saved up enough money to rent a little one bed near the station. You'd be proud dad, I put all the furniture together myself even put up a few bookshelves too.

HARI   Furniture.

MAX   Bookshelves.

NICK   I've had Paul and Laurie round – they said it was even nicer than Amy's flat.

HARI   I don't know what to say.

NICK   Say you'll come round for dinner maybe? My treat?

MAX   Of course. Of course we will.

NICK   I thought you might tell me to go away and never come back. I thought after last time you might not want anything to do with me.

MAX   Never.

HARI   Never.

NICK   I thought you might have said to each other

Pause.

239

HARI	What?
MAX	What did you think we'd have said?
NICK	I thought you might have said enough is enough. I thought you might have said you've been through so much that you couldn't do it again.
HARI	No
NICK	I thought you might have said that if I ever came back you'd tell me that you were cutting me out of your lives for good.
MAX	We wouldn't do that. We would never give up on you Nick.
HARI	No.
NICK	I'd understand Mum. I'd understand if you had done.
	Pause.
MAX	So what are you making us for this dinner?
NICK	How does lamb sound?
MAX	Yum.
HARI	What with?
NICK	Potatoes
HARI	Ooh
NICK	And greens
HARI	Delish
NICK	And swimming.
	Beat.
HARI	And what?

JÅN	And swimming.
MAX	Swimming?
JÅN	Swimming swimming swimming swimming swimming swimmi

Beep. JÅN pauses, alive but unspeaking. Silence.

MAX   I had a dream last night. I was here, in the
house, but the layout of the rooms was different.
There were new corridors and landings where
I had no idea we had even applied for planning
permission. They house seemed to go on
and on, doors and landings and towers and
stairways I couldn't find the end of it. In some
rooms were things I recognised, the fireplace,
the ultrasonic humidifier, but others opened
up to new rooms wonderful and strange. I
opened a door and saw the ocean stretched
out in front of me. I climbed into the attic and
a whole forest had grown. Inside the airing
cupboard was packed the whole universe. I
stood at the door and watched it float. As I
made my way downstairs I realised that the
ground floor must be medieval; the floors
were red brick. Everywhere it was gloomy and
dark. I came upon a heavy door and when I
opened it I discovered a stone stairway, leading
down into the depths. I descended as far as it
would go, past cellars and caverns I had never
seen before. These must be the foundations
of the house I thought. How funny that I've
never been down here. At the very bottom
of the stairs was a cave cut into the rock. To
think that this was beneath our feet the whole
time we've lived here. Thick dust lay on the
floor and in the dust were scattered stones and

broken shards of pottery, as if discarded by some primitive culture. As I lent in, getting to my hands and knees to examine more closely, I realised that these weren't bits of pottery at all. They were bones. I picked up a skull from the pile but, just as I began to turn it around to face me, I woke up.

HARI   I dreamt I was batting at number five for Middlesex.

Beep.

JÅN   I thought you might tell me to go away and never come back. I thought after last time you might not want anything to do with me me me me me me.

Beep. JÅN pauses.

MAX   How did it go with the engineer?

HARI   He said these things are cheap as chips. They go wrong all the time and the truth is no one knows why. Give him another chance and if it keeps happening then

MAX   What?

HARI   Get rid.

Dining Room

Night. MAX and NICK are talking. NICK looks worse than we've ever seen him.

NICK   Where's Dad?

MAX   Your father's upstairs.

NICK	I'd like to see him.
MAX	No.
NICK	No?
MAX	That's not a good idea.
NICK	I'm sorry I upset you. I just needed to get it out of my system but now I can focus on getting better. If I can put the deposit down on this flat I I need to explain it to Dad.
MAX	That's not going to happen.
NICK	He'll understand. I need to talk to him.
MAX	Nick. You're talking to me.
	Silence.
NICK	I made a mistake
MAX	No
NICK	I know I fucked up but can't we
MAX	Nick
NICK	I'm just asking for help
MAX	Please
NICK	Just a bit of help. I needed to fuck up to know what I need to do now
MAX	We're not going to help you this time.
NICK	Let me
MAX	We're not going to lend you any money or help you out with this flat. We're not going to let you stay here again.
NICK	I'm not asking

MAX	We're not paying for another rehab, we're not borrowing more money just so you can
NICK	I'll pay it ba
MAX	We've tried and tried but now you're on you're
NICK	I want to speak to Dad.
MAX	You're speaking to Mum! Okay? You're speaking to Mum. And she's telling you – it's over.

Silence.

MAX	If you check yourself in somewhere then maybe
NICK	You want me to be perfect
MAX	We'll try to be involved
NICK	You want me to be pristine and clean and have no scratches
MAX	If you've made that decision yourself
NICK	But that's not what people are like
MAX	Not financially but we could visit
NICK	I don't want fixing. I don't need it.
MAX	Yes you do.
NICK	I like how I am.
MAX	No you don't. You're dirty and you stink and your eyes are sunken into your head.
NICK	You don't know anything.
MAX	You're unwell.
NICK	So?
MAX	You're miserable.

NICK	No.
MAX	You're wretched.
NICK	That's what you need to think. You need to think I'm ill because you can't understand that I might have chosen this. You're scared because I might have chosen something different to you and Dad. You're scared because you're starting to realise that maybe I actually know what's going on. Maybe I've walked through this house, seen the TV room, seen the nice garden, seen the clean fridge and thought, you know what, I'd rather be high.
MAX	No.
NICK	That I would willingly sacrifice all this to be high.
MAX	No.
NICK	You think I don't know what I'm doing. But if I could go back to the very first time and I could see exactly what it would do to me, where I'd end up, how much I'd lose, I'd take it in a second. Every single time.
	Silence.
MAX	We're not going to help you this time Nick.
NICK	I want to speak to Dad.
MAX	No. This is the end.

5

Dining Room

MAX, HARI, JÅN, LAURIE, PAUL and AMY are having dinner. They eat in comfortable silence.

JÅN wipes his mouth with a napkin neatly. LAURIE and PAUL glance at JÅN, impressed. HARI and MAX share a smile, proud.

JÅN	This is delicious Dad thank you so much.
HARI	Yes it's come out quite well in the end I have to say.
	LAURIE and PAUL look at MAX like 'what a polite boy!'
JÅN	Can I pour anyone some water?
AMY	Thank you.
PAUL	I could get used to this kind of service!
JÅN	It's no trouble.
	He pours the water and they smile, impressed.
HARI	So you're down for the weekend are you Amy?
AMY	Yeah. Going back tomorrow.
MAX	And how's it going up there?
AMY	Yeah okay thanks.
LAURIE	She's loving it.
AMY	It's hard work but yeah it's what I want to do I guess so
LAURIE	She's in the Freshers play.
AMY	Mum.
MAX	Is she indeed?
LAURIE	I warned her you'll be worn out but what did you say to me Amy?

247

AMY	It doesn't matter.
LAURIE	She said 'that's what Pro Plus is for'!
AMY	It was a joke.
PAUL	In our day we took drugs to *avoid* work – isn't that right Hari?
MAX	Very admirable.
LAURIE	She's burning the candle at both ends you see because she's got her heart set on neurology.
AMY	Mum that's literally years
MAX	Neurology!
LAURIE	I'd always fancied neurology myself but never quite had the guts to go for it so I'm just thrilled that Amy has.
HARI	Must be terribly competitive.
PAUL	One in a hundred roughly.
LAURIE	And that's only including medical students of course.
HARI	Yes of course.
LAURIE	So think of all the ones who didn't even get into medical school.
AMY	Oh my god.
PAUL	You're looking at extremely long odds.
JÅN	Well very best of luck.
HARI	I remember you sitting at this table going at your pasta with a knife *reee reee reee* I didn't think then I'd fancy have you open my head up!
MAX	Hari.

LAURIE	And she's got a bloke as well.
AMY	Mum why?
LAURIE	Adam. But everyone calls him Coops.
PAUL	His name's Cooper.
AMY	And his phone number's 079
LAURIE	They asked!
AMY	Can we change the subject?
LAURIE	How about you Jån, how do you spend your days?
PAUL	Apart from helping out these old codgers!
JÅN	I'm looking for a course at the moment actually. Trying to go to University.
AMY	University? Right, is that-?
LAURIE	Do you have an idea what you'd like to study?
JÅN	I'm doing pretty well at most subjects but I think my real passion lies in management and hospitality.
PAUL	Nice. Lots of good jobs out there in that kind of field.
HARI	Exactly what I told him.
JÅN	When Dad applied to Uni he didn't really know what to do so just kind of fell into education. I don't want to make that mistake.
LAURIE	Is that true Hari?
HARI	In a manner of speaking yes. I always thought I'd be really good at running a restaurant, you know I have a passion for food.
AMY	The lamb is really lovely by the way.

249

HARI	Fancied myself starting a sort of café then maybe building it up into a little franchise you know.
PAUL	Sounds a bit more interesting than making sure year 10 have their shirts tucked in.
HARI	Still no regrets.
PAUL	No quite.
HARI	But I'm glad that Jån wants to follow that passion.
LAURIE	Nice to see him take after you.
JÅN	I'd also like to do a design subsid. Or maybe do an evening course in design.
LAURIE	Ooh taking after Max now.
MAX	Stop it I'll blush.
JÅN	I think the design of a space is so important. Even room by room it frames the way we interact with the world. The right choice of chair or curve of a frame can genuinely alter our mood. It's a reflection of who we are.
MAX	I couldn't agree more.
LAURIE	Fascinating.

LAURIE gives MAX a raised eyebrow, impressed.

HARI	And actually Jån's got a little girlfriend too, haven't you Jån?
JÅN	It's not serious.
PAUL	Take my advice Jån, you never know it's serious until it's too late!
JÅN	Well we've just started seeing each other really.

PAUL	How did you meet?
JÅN	She's a prostitute working out of Reading.
PAUL	Excuse me?
MAX	You didn't tell us that Jån.
JÅN	Oh, didn't I? Yes we met on one of my visits to that brothel.
HARI	Er Jån I'm not sure
JÅN	I'd been a few times before but I'd not really fallen for any of the other girls particularly. But then when I met Danika and we got talking I just thought yes I could really go for this girl.
PAUL	Well I suppose that's sort of sweet in a way. What was it you liked about her?
MAX	I don't think we need to
JÅN	Well she looks really young for a start, like sort of fifteen or so. And she said she'd be happy to do anal if I paid her extra. I like anal because it's a tighter hole but some of the girls are a bit reluctant
HARI	Alright mate I think that's enough.
JÅN	Oh.
MAX	It's not really dinner table talk okay darling.
JÅN	Sorry. I just wanted to tell you about this girl.
MAX	Why don't you talk about your restaurant instead, that sounds interesting?
JÅN	Okay. Well like Dad said I'd like to start small and hopefully one day expand it. I want to do sort of really low quality fried chicken and chips, that sort of place. I've had a look at the

numbers and if you buy scrap meat from the right abattoir you can save unbelievable costs, then once they're packed together in a nugget or a pie or something no one really knows the difference anyway. I think the margins are really attractive and, if I can find a location near a secondary school, I think I can really get a lot of passing trade as schools now have to serve very healthy lunches at low cost so they taste terrible and everyone goes out anyway. My dream is to one day own a fried chicken place in front of every school in England!

Beat.

LAURIE	But, aren't you worried that it might not be good for the kids?
JÅN	Sorry?
LAURIE	That, you know, they might eat too much of this stuff?
JÅN	I want them to eat too much of it. Didn't you hear the business plan? That's the whole idea.
HARI	Shall we change the subject?
JÅN	I was just trying to think of a way to make a good living. Should I not have
LAURIE	Have you guys watched the Wire?
MAX	Oh! Have we!
PAUL	Seasons three and four – mwah.
AMY	I thought season two was a bit less
HARI	But, as a body of work
LAURIE	Novelistic, actually. In my opinion it's novelistic.

252

JÅN	I actually think the Wire's overrated. Isn't it just quite boring?
	They all look at him.
AMY	These carrots are delicious Hari.
HARI	Thank you, I
JÅN	I've changed my mind. I'm sorry about before, I was being stupid. About the chicken and Danika and stuff. I don't really love Danika, I was only joking. And of course the Wire is brilliant. It's the closest thing this century has to Dickensian social observation.
HARI	Okay, that's better.
MAX	He does this you see, he's always trying to self-improve.
JÅN	And the chicken was a stupid idea. I think I'd rather sell organic tacos with a vegan twist.
LAURIE	That sounds lovely.
JÅN	Or Moroccan influenced burritos.
PAUL	Mmmm.
JÅN	Or locally sourced chutneys. I haven't decided yet. But I know I want it to be good. I want it to be successful. But I don't just mean financially; the most important thing is the quality of the work
PAUL	Wow, he's got his head screwed on – no pun intended Hari.
JÅN	But in fact the quality of the work is just a route not a destination. The destination is the pride I will take from the work itself. And the pride I'll take from the pride you'll take in me.

LAURIE	Gosh.
AMY	Is he
JÅN	There is a pride in work and a pride in produce. I know that certain products are better than others. An apple is better than a cigarette. A toaster is better than a bong. A netball is better than a beer can. I want to surround myself with good things. I want to take pride in my surroundings. I want to learn and be better and I think I am, I'm trying anyway
HARI	*(Starting to sense a growing mania.)* Would anyone like a coffee? Jån shall we
JÅN	Because that is the most important thing: happiness. Mental wellbeing. I know that I want to grow old and wise one day. I want to be full of pride and satisfaction and happiness. But not the wrong kind of happiness.
HARI	Jån.
JÅN	Not artificial happiness, but organic happiness. I know from Mum and Dad that that's all they want.
LAURIE	That's… sweet.
HARI	Let's change the subject shall we?
LAURIE	Amy why don't you tell them about the film society you
JÅN	I'd like to be a human rights lawyer one day.
HARI	Okay Jån.
JAN	I'd like to take a year out to work for an NGO.
MAX	Jan.

JÅN	I'd like to write novels that subtly reflect the contemporary condition.
AMY	Maybe we should
JÅN	I'd like to marry Amy!
HARI	*(Trying to cover.)* Ah, that's a sweet thought Jån.
JÅN	Yes yes yes I'd like the two of us to have the kind of happiness that she and Coops have now.
AMY	Mum?
JÅN	That's what I want. I want to be the kind of guy that Amy likes. The kind of guy that Paul and Laurie likes.
LAURIE	We do –

JÅN grabs AMY by the arm.

AMY	Ah!
JÅN	I want me and Amy to get married and move back here to live really nearby
AMY	Get off Jån.
MAX	Jån let her go.
JÅN	*(Dragging her to her feet.)* I want us to have children and be a happy family just like all of you guys.
AMY	Ah – Hari tell him to
PAUL	Jån get off, do you understand, get off her.
JÅN	I want us to have beautiful perfect children that we will love

He pushes her down onto the table, standing over her, wrestling with her arms. The adults scream and stand,

255

shocked. JÅN begins to pull at her skirt, fumble with his fly as PAUL and HARI jump in.

AMY   What the fuck are you

PAUL   Hey!

AMY   Ah!

HARI   Jån!

HARI and PAUL wrestle JÅN from AMY, calming him down. AMY scrabbles up from the table towards the door, away from them all.

MAX   Amy I I'm sorry I

AMY looks at MAX. Pause. AMY collects her bag from her chair and goes to the door. She turns to face MAX again.

AMY   I'm really sorry about Nick, Max. I miss him.
        I didn't know him well but I looked up to him
        a lot and I really I really liked him. He was the
        guy who was older than me I don't know if that
        means anything to you but it meant a lot to me.
        He was always the year ahead, always a few
        steps ahead and now and soon and this year I'll
        overtake him and that's made me really sad. I
        wanted to come here today to tell you that to
        tell you how great I thought Nick was. Thank
        you for a lovely dinner.

AMY goes.

LAURIE Come on Paul.

JÅN   I'm sorry. I was trying trying to be good.

MAX   No, don't go. You don't have to go.

JÅN   Sorry sorry sorry

MAX	We can laugh about this. This is stupid really. Hari, say something.
HARI	Would anyone like a fruit tea?
LAURIE	Paul, now.
	They begin to gather their things.
MAX	Laurie please. Don't go.
JÅN	I'm trying to be polite Mum. I I'm – Laurie you look really nice this evening.
LAURIE	Paul!
JÅN	That shirt is a lovely colour on you.
MAX	He can be good, I promise. Jån say something nice.
JÅN	I fantasise about your lips on my cock.
HARI	Jesus Christ
PAUL	Right that's it.
JÅN	I'm sorry Paul, is that offensive?
LAURIE	Thanks Hari, thanks Max.
JÅN	It's okay Paul, I fantasise about your lips on my cock too.
MAX	Jån!
HARI	Guys wait, he doesn't mean it, you don't need to rush off.
PAUL	We said we'd Skype with Cal when we got back. He's on a training camp in Australia so the time difference, you know.
JÅN	I'm sorry I'm sorry I'm sorry I ruined it. Don't go please don't go I can do better I promise I can do better.

257

LAURIE	Goodbye Hari.
JÅN	I want to be the CEO of a huge company.
PAUL	Bye Max.
JÅN	I want to be the editor of a national newspaper.
MAX	Please

PAUL and LAURIE go. HARI follows after them.

JÅN	I want to have a job I want to have a conversation I want to have a bath I just want to be able to have a bath tomorrow I want to
MAX	Jån!
HARI	*(Off.)* Paul! Laurie! Come on, there's no need to go.
JÅN	I'm so sorry.
MAX	Don't.
JÅN	Mum?
MAX	Oh Jån.
JÅN	Mum Mum Mum Mum Mum Mum
MAX	No Jån.
JÅN	Mum Mum Mum Mum
MAX	Jån?

Front Garden

HARI	Paul wait!
PAUL	Sorry mate it's just Cal's waiting you know and it's all got a bit

LAURIE	*(Off.)* Paul!
PAUL	Yeah coming love.
HARI	It's only a blip. Honestly give me five minutes with a screwdriver I'm telling you he'll be right as rain. Please mate just come back inside. For Max. She was really excited about tonight. She just wanted to show we just wanted
LAURIE	*(Off.)* Paul!
HARI	We just wanted you to be impressed with him.
PAUL	Hari, I don't know how to say this but, the boy's a machine okay. Even before he had his little meltdown it's a bit. I mean all that looking to the future stuff, university, getting a job, isn't it a bit, it's a bit weird.
HARI	Wh-? What do you mean?
PAUL	We went along with it when it was a bit of fun when it was inside the house but this is is
HARI	What?
PAUL	It's like you're actually raising him or something. Like a, I mean, why bother? What's it all for?
HARI	For… love.

The sound of a car engine starts.

| PAUL | I'll see you soon alright Hari. |

PAUL goes. The sound of a car leaving. HARI watches it disappear down the street. Then, a huge banging noise comes from the house.

Destroyed Hallway

MAX	Hari, Hari!
HARI	Right where is he?
MAX	Something's malfunctioned I couldn't turn him off
HARI	Where is he?
MAX	I tried fiddling with the remote but the damned thing has so many functions
HARI	Max
MAX	You're never in the right mode
HARI	Max
MAX	And then if you are in the mode you've not got them on the right setting
HARI	Max!
MAX	I couldn't control him. I'm sorry.
HARI	I've only walked them to their car what on earth's happened?
MAX	He was shaken he was out of control stuck in some sort of malfunction I I I couldn't – he ran into the living room
HARI	Keep calm.
MAX	I followed. I tried to soothe him
HARI	And
MAX	And he's st st staring at the wall like I said moaning. I should have I don't know I didn't know what to do Hari I didn't know what to do
HARI	Did he hurt you?

MAX	He was just moaning I was trying to speak to him but I couldn't I couldn't
HARI	It's okay
MAX	He wouldn't listen nothing was getting through. I reached for the remote but before I could do anything he just switches. I was scared.

Destroyed Sitting Room

MAX	He picked up the television. Smashed it against the wall and the cables all ripped out of the sockets. Glass flew everywhere. I had to duck behind the sofa for cover. I scrambled for the remote but it had got mixed up with all the DVD ones and the Sonos thing and
HARI	It's got a little red label that's why I made the labels.
MAX	I couldn't read the labels could I because Jån was smashing the room to smithereens by using the lamp as a makeshift baseball bat! I was fumbling trying to find the right one, trying to calm him down but it was no good. I followed him back to the kitchen.

Destroyed Kitchen

MAX	But he had already got to the fridge pulling everything out emptying the veg tray.
HARI	Oh Max.
MAX	He was screaming and shouting.

| HARI | What on earth about? |
| MAX | About nonsense about nothing about nonsense stuff. He's got this look in his eyes like he's just gone like his wiring's just gone and there I am banging away at those stupid buttons as he smashes through the conservatory, |

Destroyed Conservatory

| MAX | Rampaging through my pots and ripping up the flowers, back inside, into the hall |

Destroyed Hall

MAX	Pulling the photos off the wall and smashing them against the paint.
HARI	This is supposed to be a premium product
MAX	I'd almost given up on the remote I was trying to reason with him
HARI	Never in my life
MAX	Find out what was on his mind. But he was already upstairs.

Destroyed Bed

| MAX | Crashing into things |

Destroyed Bathroom

MAX   Tearing rooms apart

Destroyed Study

MAX   It was like a madman in the house it was like

HARI   Don't Max

MAX   It was like

HARI   My printer!

Destroyed Landing

MAX   Eventually he ended up here. Closed the door and hasn't come out since.

      Silence.

HARI   Do you still have the remote?

      She hands it over.

HARI   You see here's the label it's very clear.

      Death stare.

HARI   But yes of course you were under pressure so fair enough. Right.

      He knocks. No answer.

HARI   Jån? You're not in any trouble. We just want to talk.

      Silence.

HARI   Jån mate we're going to come in alright?

Teenage Boy's Room

JÅN has let them in. It's a teenage boy's room, as messy as the day it was left. Silence.

HARI   Haven't been up here for a while.

MAX   No.

HARI   We keep meaning to get it cleaned up don't we?

MAX   Yes.

HARI   Should get a zipvan or something, just blitz it one weekend. I could ask Tone if he fancies giving us a hand actually.

JÅN   I could give you a hand.

HARI   What were we talking about a few months ago Max, a study for you?

MAX   A gym.

HARI   That's right a gym.

She nods. Silence.

HARI   So.

MAX nods.

JÅN   I'm sorry I hurt Amy. I'm sorry I ruined the dinner party. I didn't mean to I don't know what. I don't know why I. It won't happen again.

HARI gestures to give him his hand. JÅN holds out his hand. HARI takes it.

HARI   I'm sorry Jån.

He begins to unscrew his left hand.

JÅN   It won't. I promise it won't.

264

HARI continues to screw.

JÅN	Please.
MAX	Give me your hand love.
JÅN	Mum.
MAX	Here, give me your hand.

MAX takes his other hand in hers.

JÅN	Dad.
MAX	That's it.
JÅN	Please don't do this.
HARI	It's okay.
JÅN	I don't know what happened. I'll try again let's try again.
HARI	I'm sorry Jan.
JÅN	I promise.

The hands come off. They begin to untwist the elbows.

JÅN	Dad don't please please I promise. I can do better I will I'll do better. I must have short circuited or something some kind of processing problem or a software malfunction. Don't do this Mum. Please don't give up on me. Please don't
MAX	It's okay love.

And now the shoulders.

JÅN	Please

JÅN's arm comes loose with a gaggle of wires hanging loose at the join.

HARI	Jån listen to me. You've been fantastic for us, and we've loved having you. But Max and I saw something, a particular something, with certain specifications and certain guarantees of quality and unfortunately – it's not your fault – but it's just not been quite what we were expecting.
	HARI reaches for the back of JÅN's head.
JÅN	Was I broken from the start do you think?
	They look at him.
HARI	I don't know love. I'm sorry.
	They turn him off and he crumples to the floor. MAX and HARI stand in silence, surrounded by the carnage of their child, parts of his body scattered around the room.
	MAX holds up JÅN's separated hand and stares at it.
MAX	I'm sorry.
HARI	It's not your fault, the remote was
MAX	Not him. Not him.
	Silence.
MAX	That night when he came to me.
HARI	I should have joined you.
MAX	And I turned him away.
HARI	I should have supported you.
MAX	How could a mother do that?
HARI	We both decided. I mean that Max we both
MAX	How could a mother give up?
HARI	We thought it was the only way.

MAX	That was the last time he was here. It was only a couple of weeks before he. And when he was at the door. When I was showing him out that night and I saw he had a cut on his finger.

MAX looks at the hand she's holding.

MAX	It wasn't even a bad one, and God knows he'd had some scratches on him over the years. He held it up to me and it was like he was just a kid again. A little kid with a scratch. And I took his finger in my hand, an adult's hand, a man's hand now, all dirty and grimy and and and I kissed it better. And you know what? I thought it would work. I thought in that moment, as I said goodbye, I thought that little kiss would make that finger better, just like when he was five.
HARI	Maybe it did? Maybe that finger got better. But there are so many parts. So many parts deep inside that we couldn't get to.
MAX	Yes.

She drops the hand. Silence.

MAX	I don't know if I can face it Hari. I don't know if I can.
HARI	I know.
MAX	I just want to feel better.
HARI	I know. I know.

Silence. He holds her. He looks at what's left of JÅN and loosens his grip. She regains her composure and notices JÅN too. They stare at him. And as they stare, a thought begins to crystallise in their minds. A thought as clean and pristine as a flatpacked wardrobe.

MAX	Straight lines.
	Silence.
HARI	It wouldn't be that hard. The truth is most of this is just casing. In theory there's no reason you couldn't
MAX	Uh huh.
HARI	Slide it in and hook it up
MAX	Because I'm finding mine so messy.
HARI	Me too.
MAX	It's tiring me out.
HARI	I wake up in the night do you?
MAX	Yes.
HARI	I wake up and I've just got so many
MAX	Yes
HARI	Thoughts.
MAX	Me too.
HARI	It's tiring.
MAX	I'd love
HARI	Oh god I'd love
MAX	A good night's sleep.
	Pause.
MAX	The world can never be perfect that's not going to happen.
	HARI shakes his head.
MAX	But we can.
	They look at each other.

HARI	I'll get the instruction manual.
	HARI goes. MAX looks at JÅN.
	HARI reappears with the manual, held open.
HARI	Here we are. There, if you get started on me then once you're done, I can do you.
MAX	Right: To boot into a basic alternative shell or prefabricated organism rather than launching the provided SKIN_GUI, you will need: a scalpel (sterilized), strong thread, belt or ratchet straps and clamps (sterilized) in addition to the provided BORN_setup_pack.
HARI	Right you are. I'll pop to the toolshed.
MAX	Okay. I might lay out a towel, just don't want to dirty the carpet.
HARI	Good idea.
MAX	Unless
HARI	What?
	Pause.
MAX	No I was just thinking
HARI	Yes perhaps you're right.
	Pause.
MAX	We're being silly aren't we?
HARI	I think I just got carried away.
MAX	That was nearly a very stupid mistake.
HARI	We should just do it in the bathroom.
MAX	Then we can wipe down the surfaces and it'll only take a few seconds.
HARI	I'll meet you there.

Ensuite Bathroom

Lots of blood on the floor. A bandage on HARI's head.

MAX	How do you feel?
HARI	A little queasy.
MAX	But?
HARI	Good. I feel good. Great actually.

HARI looks at himself, feels himself, blinks in this new dawn.

HARI	Right, your turn.
MAX	Great.
HARI	Oh damnit!
MAX	What?
HARI	The spare CPU chip, it's been sitting here in the blood.
MAX	Oh bugger.
HARI	It's totally soaked.

Pause.

HARI	I could pop to the shop.
MAX	Oh but that's a fag.
HARI	And it'll be closed at this time of night. (*He thinks.*) We could order it online?
MAX	Yes.
HARI	It'll be here tomorrow if we do it now.
MAX	Another night (*to endure*).
HARI	Hmm.

MAX	Well I suppose we don't have a choice.
HARI	Unless.
MAX	What?
HARI	Of course! I should have thought of this before. I'll pop to the attic and fish the circuit board out of that old fax machine.
MAX	Oh.
HARI	Once it's soldered onto the dry part of this should be right as rain. I knew it would come in useful.
MAX	Do you think it will be powerful enough?
HARI	Oh I'll augment it with some of the leftover pins we've still got in the pack.
MAX	Leftover
HARI	And boost the power with the battery pack from my electric toothbrush.
MAX	Right.
HARI	I should think it'll do fine. Back in a tick.
MAX	Okay, I'll wait here.

He goes. MAX is alone. She waits in silence, impassive. She picks up the instructions, looks at them, and puts them down. She picks up the toothbrush. Silence.

Ensuite Bathroom

Empty. HARI returns, holding the fax machine. He sees that the room is empty.

| HARI | Max? |

He looks in the bath. Not there. Pause.

HARI   Max?

Kitchen

HARI   Max?

Living Room

HARI   Darling?

Conservatory

HARI   Lovie?

Study

HARI   Love?

Teenage Boy's Bedroom

HARI   There you are. I couldn't find you anywhere.

MAX   Were you worried?

          Pause.

HARI   *(Pleased.)* No.

MAX   Not at all?

HARI	No. Just sort of… curious.
MAX	That sounds good.
	Silence.
HARI	I found the fax. It's downstairs in the bathroom.
MAX	Okay.
HARI	Shouldn't take a sec to whizz out the circuit board for you.
MAX	Great.
HARI	Shall we go then?
MAX	Yes.
	She doesn't move.
MAX	Does it feel nice?
HARI	It's wonderful actually. Plus.
MAX	Yes?
HARI	I disabled my sense of smell. So no more Wednesday night bin night worries.
MAX	That will be a relief.
HARI	And I've turned down my hearing too. So everything's just a little more
MAX	Mm?
HARI	Peaceful.
MAX	Hari?
HARI	Yes?
MAX	I don't think I want to do it. At least not tonight.
HARI	What? Why not?
	MAX doesn't answer.

273

HARI	We can use *your* toothbrush if you'd prefer?
	Pause.
HARI	We've always tried to fix things haven't we? It's a point of pride. If things are broken I don't see the harm in giving them a bit of a polish or a refit.
MAX	I suppose.
HARI	I know some people have the attitude that maybe we should all feel guilty or torture ourselves or that a bit of darkness lets you know that there's light etc. etc. I know all that. But my feeling is: wouldn't it be better if it was just always light? The fact is you only live once. And do you want to spend that time being a worry wart and moping about or would you rather get up and go and be able to enjoy things a bit more? This way is just
MAX	Nicer.
HARI	Exactly. So. Are you coming downstairs?
	A long pause. MAX takes a deep breath.
MAX	Yes.

Hallway

MAX and NICK are in the hallway saying a final, awkward goodbye.

NICK	I'll see you soon okay.
	MAX nods.
NICK	I'm telling you I can do this on my own.
	Pause.
NICK	I'm going to do it.

274

MAX	You should go.
NICK	Say goodbye to Dad from me though yeah.
	MAX nods. She opens the door.
NICK	It's pissing down. Fuck.
MAX	You should go.
NICK	I didn't bring a coat. Fuck.
	They look at each other. NICK knows it's time to go. He reaches down for his bag.
MAX	Your finger. It's bleeding.
	NICK looks at his finger.
NICK	Hardly. It's nothing.
	MAX takes his hand and looks at it.
MAX	Is it sore?
	NICK shakes his head. MAX stares at the tiny cut, barely visible. She strokes it with her hand and looks again at NICK. She holds the hand tight and looks again at the finger. She brings it to her lips and kisses the cut better.
MAX	There. All better.
	NICK smiles.
NICK	Yeah. All better.

6

Gym

A new day, some time later. They run on treadmills.

HARI	How do you feel?
MAX	Great I feel great.
HARI	Me too.
MAX	Tired.
HARI	Me too.
MAX	But great.
HARI	Here.
MAX	Thanks.
HARI	Don't finish it though as I need to keep hydrated.
MAX	There you go.
HARI	Thanks. Looks good no?
MAX	Looks great
HARI	I knew we could get two of the cross trainers in here.
MAX	It was worth taking off the base to get them up the stairs though.
HARI	Definitely.
MAX	Otherwise we'd have struggled.
HARI	But now I think with these two in
MAX	Maybe a pull-up bar on the door
HARI	Maybe a pull-up bar on the door. And your yoga mats brought up
MAX	That would be nice.
HARI	I would say it's just about perfect.
	They run and run and run.
	The end.

WWW.OBERONBOOKS.COM